Annual Survey

UK Government & Politics

Paul Fairclough
Richard Kelly
Eric Magee

Philip Allan Updates
Market Place
Deddington
OX15 0SE

Orders

Bookpoint Ltd, 130 Milton Park, Abingdon, Oxfordshire, OX14 4SB
tel: 01235 827720
fax: 01235 400454
e-mail: uk.orders@bookpoint.co.uk

Lines are open 9.00 a.m.–5.00 p.m., Monday to Saturday, with a 24-hour
message answering service. You can also order through the Philip Allan
Updates website: www.philipallan.co.uk

Printed by Raithby, Lawrence & Co Ltd, Leicester

Environmental information
The paper on which this title is printed is sourced from managed, sustainable
forests.

Contents

Chapter 1

Blair's leadership challenged: 'cock-up' or conspiracy?

About this chapter

At the beginning of September 2006, Tony Blair faced an open revolt over his failure to say when he would hand over power to his successor. This chapter places these events in context and answers the following questions:

- How close did Tony Blair come to leaving Number 10 in 2006?
- How had the Labour Party become so divided over the leadership issue?
- Who are the possible contenders to succeed Blair?
- Will a new leader result in a change in either style or substance for the government?

How close did Blair come to leaving Number 10 in 2006?

The fact that Tony Blair was still the prime minister at the time that the clocks were put back at the end of October would have come as a shock to those who had predicted — and in some cases favoured — an earlier exit for the premier.

With the UK political scene increasingly said to represent that of the dog days of the 'Major years' (see Box 1.1), the government was floored by a series of high-profile policy failures (in both the domestic and foreign spheres) and renewed allegations of sleaze, particularly in respect of the loans for peerages scandal and John Prescott's alleged abuse of privileges. By the summer of 2006, the tabloids and the broadsheets alike were rife with talk of embryonic backbench plots against the prime minister. The message to Blair was increasingly clear: name a date for the orderly handover of power to Brown or face a leadership challenge from the backbenches.

It was reported that such off-the-record musings had evolved into a fully fledged plot to oust Blair by the start of September, for reasons we will discuss later in this chapter. How serious was this 'plot'?

Box 1.1 A decade on

'A minister caught cheating on his wife, ructions in the Home Office, splits in the ruling party, a Prime Minister who is not going to be in office for much longer and a new, young opposition leader who looks like a winner. Yes, this was British politics 10 years ago.'

Source: *Independent*, 28 April 2006.

The backbench coup — 'cock-up' or conspiracy?

Blair returned from his summer break in the Caribbean at the start of September 2006 to find his party in open revolt over his failure to set a clear timetable for the orderly handover of power to his successor. Issues surrounding the succession had plagued Blair's premiership since before the 2005 general election, but matters came to a head when he once again refused to 'set a date' in an interview with *The Times* on 1 September. What followed was, by any standards, an extraordinary sequence of events (see Table 1.1).

Date	Event
1 September	Blair returns from the Caribbean, still reluctant to name the date on which he will leave Number 10.
3 September	Byers and Milburn put pressure on Brown. Brownites threaten a formal leadership challenge to Blair.
4 September	80 Labour MPs are ready to sign one of the letters circulating at parliament that call for Blair's resignation.
5 September	Loyal Blairites are said to be looking for an exit strategy for the prime minister.
6 September	Blair and Brown are engaged in a $3\frac{1}{2}$-hour shouting match over the succession. Minister Tom Watson and six parliamentary private secretaries resign over their opposition to the prime minister.
7 September	Blair apologises to the public for the events over the preceding 4 days, admitting that 'it has not been our finest hour' and confirming that the 2006 Party Conference would be his last as leader.

Table 1.1 The anatomy of a Labour leadership coup

First, former Blairite cabinet ministers Stephen Byers and Alan Milburn appeared in the press calling for Gordon Brown to set out a clearer vision regarding where he intended to take the party as leader. Crucially, they called for the chancellor to make an explicit commitment to holding to the Blair agenda on public-service reform. At the same time, Brown's supporters were briefing that there might be a formal leadership challenge to the prime minister unless he moved quickly to set a departure date.

A day later, on 4 September, it emerged that a number of letters calling for Blair's resignation had been circulating among Labour MPs, with around 80 said to be willing to add their signatures to calls for the prime minister to stand down with immediate effect. The sense that even Blair's supporters were looking for an exit strategy was heightened by reports that one of the letters was coordinated by Blairites Sion Simon and Chris Bryant, and also by documents leaked to the *Daily Mirror* suggesting that insiders were set to smooth Blair's exit from Number 10 with a series of 'feel-good' appearances on television programmes such as *Blue Peter* and *Songs of Praise*.

By the time Brown met with Blair at Downing Street on 6 September, the chancellor and the prime minister were said to be in open warfare. The

Guardian reported that the meeting, which lasted over 3 hours, had descended into a 'shouting match', with Brown demanding that Blair silence those who had been briefing against him (in particular, Byers and Milburn) and also that Blair should commit to leaving office by Christmas 2006. The resignation of defence minister Tom Watson, a signatory to another of the letters (whom Blair described as 'disloyal, discourteous and wrong'), and six parliamentary private secretaries on the same day appeared to leave the prime minister in a desperate situation — a sense that was given added weight by a snapshot of a grinning Brown caught as he was being chauffeured away from Number 10 at the end of his meeting with Blair.

It was surprising, therefore, that the tension appeared to dissipate after this point. Though the prime minister's announcement on 7 September that he would go within the year did not appear to have silenced those who wanted a speedier end to his tenure, the situation had become calmer by the end of the Labour Party Conference on 28 September.

Why was this? Some have suggested that the way in which the crisis appeared to pass almost as quickly as it had emerged reflected the extent to which all of those involved could see the damage being done to the party's electoral prospects. Intra-party divisions had certainly played their part in Labour spending 18 years in opposition between 1979 and 1997. The prime minister's words on 7 September (see Table 1.1) appeared to reflect a more generally held view that the party was in danger of throwing away the reputation for unity that it had fought so hard to establish.

Some suggested that the failure of the plot might have had just as much to do with the fact that Brown did not throw his full weight behind those seeking to force the prime minister out. Much of the press attention centred on the fact that Tom Watson had visited Brown in his Fife home on the weekend before the letters started to circulate. However, while few took at face value Watson's claim that the two families had simply 'watched a *Postman Pat* video on a DVD and played with their babies', most remained unconvinced that this had been a fully fledged Brownite coup. Surely, they argued, a real coup would have seen far more ministerial resignations and an even bigger impetus from the chancellor's backbench supporters? Perhaps, therefore, the long-term favourite to succeed Blair did not himself think that the time was right, despite his apparent pleasure at the prime minister's discomfort.

How had it got to this point?

Blair's self-confessed error in announcing his departure

Blair's decision, in the run-up to the 2005 general election, to 'pre-announce' his planned departure from Number 10 had the effect of creating a kind of limbo, or ministerial paralysis, at the heart of government. With media attention inevitably focused on when Blair would go and who might replace him, the prime minister was unable to manage the media agenda in the style that characterised New Labour's first term. Cabinet colleagues were equally torn, on the one hand needing to run their departments with the necessary rigour, and on the other feeling compelled to have one eye on their political futures.

The prime minister appeared to acknowledge that he had made a mistake in an interview with the Australian broadcaster ABC, reported in the *Independent* on 27 March. According to the paper's political editor, Andrew Grice, Blair had accepted that while his intention in making the announcement had been to prevent his third term being 'overshadowed by media speculation' surrounding his future — and also to reassure Gordon Brown that he would not be seeking a fourth term as leader — the announcement had fuelled, as opposed to extinguished, the media's curiosity.

Blair's manner and behaviour

By 2006, Blair's behaviour in office was giving some of his backbenchers genuine cause for concern. First, there was the accusation that his centralising tendencies — the alleged 'control freakery' observed by former colleagues such as the late Mo Mowlam — remained undiminished. This despite assurances that the prime minister had given to the parliamentary Labour Party after it had been bloodied (though not defeated) in the 2005 general election.

Second, the prime minister's reluctance to admit fundamental mistakes over Iraq and his apparent willingness to stand shoulder to shoulder with the USA over the Israeli invasion of Lebanon did little to reassure those who felt that Blair had lost the ability to tap into the national *Zeitgeist*.

Brown's impatience

The Blair–Brown double act is normally said to date from the 1994 Granita pact, where the two men supposedly met at the London restaurant in order to carve up the Labour leadership between themselves. It was agreed that Blair would take the top job. Brown would be chancellor of the exchequer, with the lure of significant influence over other departmental areas and a promise that he would become prime minister during New Labour's second term in office. If such a promise was indeed made, it is entirely understandable that Brown might indeed have grown impatient by September 2006, 18 months into New Labour's third term.

Policy failures

Though governments that have been in office for some time commonly have problems in respect of their policy agendas — witness the decline of the Conservatives in the 1990s — one would have expected a Labour government with a workable Commons majority to make greater headway. Instead, in 2006, Blair's government faced a series of increasingly embarrassing debacles across the full breadth of its programme. Domestically, the third-term education reforms faced significant opposition, ultimately being passed only as a result of the support given by Conservative MPs in the Commons. Similarly, an embarrassing series of major gaffes at the Home Office led the department's secretary of state, Charles Clarke, to resign and his replacement, John Reid, to declare that the department he had inherited was 'not fit for purpose'.

In foreign affairs also, matters appeared to be heading in one direction only. The government's refusal to use the phrase 'civil war' in reference to the situation in Iraq did little to assuage continued criticism of the UK/US-led invasion. By the end of 2006, the situation appeared to be deteriorating in Afghanistan too. The prime minister's willingness to tie himself to the US line over Lebanon also threatened to leave him isolated not only from his cabinet colleagues — most of whom went on record to criticise US support for what they felt was a disproportionate Israeli response to the Hamas threat — but also from the diplomatic service and his own foreign policy advisers. The ease with which the press was able to characterise Blair as George W. Bush's 'poodle' was particularly problematic. As early as 13 May, the *Economist* was dubbing the increasingly desperate Bush–Blair co-dependence as an 'axis of feeble'. By 3 August, 'firm of conviction, short of friends' is how the *Guardian* described Blair in his approach to dealing with the Middle Eastern crisis, as he cut an ever more desperate figure.

Sleaze, scandal and incompetence in government
The sense that Blair's third Labour administration was entering a period of terminal decline reminiscent of the dying days of the Major years was heightened by the re-emergence of sleaze, scandal and incompetence as political issues.

The embarrassment of what some journalists called 'Black Wednesday (II)' marked the beginning of a run of bad luck for New Labour. On the first 'Black Wednesday' (16 September 1992), the Conservative government lost its long-held reputation for economic competence. Fourteen years later, the events of 26 April 2006 (see Box 1.2) made the Labour government look quite ridiculous. Though the manner in which the Home Office descended into chaos after the prisoners scandal eventually forced Charles Clarke to resign, the Prescott affair was more serious for the prime minister. The media had long poked fun at Prescott's record on policy, but the deputy prime minister had always brought two key attributes to the cabinet table. First, he was seen as honest and straight-talking — an old-school bruiser who provided a counter-point to the New Labour spin and control. Second, he was the one figure who appeared able to facilitate the increasingly tense working relationship between the prime minister and his chancellor.

As the Prescott affair unravelled, it became a good deal more complex. What had initially appeared as simply an affair, morphed into a question of an abuse of privilege when it emerged that the deputy prime minister had broken civil-service rules by allowing his mistress to travel on the party's election battle bus, and had also broken a number of rules detailed in his own department's staff handbook. The sense that Prescott was fast becoming a laughing stock was aggravated by the fact that his resignation or dismissal would result in a Labour Party deputy leadership contest that would in turn reopen the debate over the timing of the election for the leadership of the party. Blair's solution — to keep Prescott on nominally as deputy prime minister while distributing his ministerial responsibilities to other cabinet members — smacked of political expediency. Though Prescott lost his much-loved grace-and-favour retreat of Dorneywood, he retained his £134,000 salary and a pension that the *Observer* reported would be worth £1.5 million should he remain in cabinet until 2010.

Box 1.2 **Black Wednesday (II)**

'It can be safely assumed that the person responsible for planning the penultimate week of Labour's efforts for the 2006 council elections did not intend to include the following: the Health Secretary being ridiculed for insisting that the NHS had enjoyed its "best year ever" and then being booed by nurses; the Home Secretary under-cutting the party's campaign over law and order and antisocial behaviour by presiding over the improper release of 1023 foreign national prisoners; and the Deputy Prime Minister (also the minister who is in charge of local government) being obliged to admit to a long sexual liaison with his secretary.'

Source: 'Black Wednesday (II) — the exposing of Clarke, Prescott and Hewitt', *The Times*, 27 April 2006.

The events of the second Black Wednesday were neither the first nor the last crises to hit the Labour government in the first half of 2006. Earlier, in February, the culture secretary, Tessa Jowell, had been drawn into the financial scandal involving her (soon-to-be estranged) husband, David Mills, and his former client, the Italian prime minister, Silvio Berlusconi. By that stage, questions were already being asked about loans made to the Labour Party before the 2005 general election. By the time the dust had settled on the events of 26 April, questions over whether these loans had broken the rules governing party funding had developed into an investigation over whether such contributions were linked to the award of peerages and other honours. Prompted by a number of opposition MPs, these questions quickly developed into a Scotland Yard investigation into the alleged sale of peerages.

At the time of writing, it was hard to assess just how damaging such allegations had been. By 11 November all those who had held cabinet office at the time of the 2005 general election had been contacted by the police about acting as possible witnesses to the alleged offence. Other key figures, Lord Levy for example, had been questioned, and it was said that it was only a matter of time before the prime minister himself was questioned. Such allegations did not play well with the public (see Box 1.3).

As noted in *Annual Survey 2006*, trust had been at the forefront of many voters' minds in the 1997 general election, not least because the closing years of John Major's administration had been dogged by allegations of sleaze following the 'cash for questions' scandal. By the time of the ICM poll for the *Sunday Telegraph* on 19 March, 73% of respondents were expressing the view that the government was 'as sleazy' or 'more sleazy' than the Conservative administration that it had swept from office 9 years before. Such results were not surprising given that a Populus poll for *The Times* had reported similar findings earlier in the month (see Table 1.2).

Is the Labour government more or less guilty of sleaze than the previous Conservative government, or do you think they are both about the same?			
	All	**Men**	**Women**
More sleazy	15%	19%	12%
Less sleazy	11%	13%	9%
About the same	67%	63%	71%

Source: *The Times*, 7 March 2006.

Table 1.2 The spectre of sleaze

Emergence of a credible opposition

Though Labour's failures over policy and the various scandals that afflicted the party in 2006 played a part in increasing the pressure on the prime minister, one should not underestimate the role played by the rejuvenation of the official opposition under the leadership of David Cameron. Though early criticism of Cameron as someone who was big on style but weak on substance might have concerned the party's elder statesmen, the new Conservative leader quickly emerged as an individual who could engage with voters — a Tory 'Blair'. Though it is probably true that William Hague remains the most effective of recent Conservative leaders at the dispatch box, Cameron has shown himself to be more than capable of exploiting the government's discomfort over issues as diverse as immigration and climate change. The presence of a credible opposition has also acted as a catalyst for unease and dissent within the Labour ranks, both inside and outside

parliament. The urgency with which Gordon Brown has sought to hammer out a timetable for the succession could also be seen as a product of the threat posed by Cameron's 'new Tories'.

Poor polls and election defeats

This sense — that matters were slipping away from Labour — was further heightened by a series of electoral disasters and spiralling poll ratings. The tone was set with the loss of the Dunfermline and West Fife by-election on 9 February. Labour's loss of the seat to the Liberal Democrats — the first Scottish by-election defeat for Labour in nearly 20 years — was a major blow in what was, and remains, a solidly working-class constituency. Labour's failure to recapture its traditional stronghold of Blaenau Gwent in a by-election that followed the death of independent Peter Law was compounded by the party being pushed into fourth place by UKIP in the by-election held in Bromley and Chislehurst on the same day.

Though in all three contests it was the Liberal Democrats rather than the Conservatives who made the most ground, such results would have sent a clear message to those Labour backbenchers nursing wafer-thin majorities.

Neither the May local elections — in which Labour suffered widespread losses (see Table 1.3) — nor the regular opinion polls would have offered the party much comfort. On 10 May, a YouGov poll for the *Daily Telegraph* confirmed Tony Blair as the most unpopular Labour prime minister ever, with only 26% satisfied with his performance, compared with 27% achieved by Harold Wilson following the devaluation of the pound in May 1968. In the same poll, 37% of those questioned said that they would vote Conservative, compared with only 31% for Labour and 17% for the Liberal Democrats. By November 2006, the Conservatives were odds-on to form the next government according to bookmakers Coral (see Table 1.4).

Party	Councillors	Change +/–
Conservative	1830	+316
Labour	1439	−319
Liberal Democrat	909	+2
Others	240	−2

Party	Councils	Change +/–
Conservative	68	+11
Labour	30	−17
Liberal Democrat	13	+1
No overall control	66	+6

Source: based on data from **http://news.bbc.co.uk/**

Table 1.3 Local election results for councils contested, 4 May 2006

Party	Odds
Conservative	4/7
Labour	5/4
Liberal Democrat	100/1

Source: odds available with bookmakers Coral on 9 November 2006.

Table 1.4 The Conservatives: 'odds-on' to win the next general election

Who was best placed to take on Blair's mantle by the end of 2006?

In November 2006, the bookmakers appeared convinced that Gordon Brown would ultimately succeed Tony Blair as Labour leader (see Table 1.5).

Contender	Odds
Gordon Brown	2/7
John Reid	6/1
Alan Johnson	6/1
David Miliband	20/1
Hilary Benn	25/1
Alan Milburn	33/1
John Hutton	33/1
Charles Clarke	50/1
Peter Hain	66/1
Jack Straw	66/1

Source: odds available with bookmakers Coral on 9 November 2006.

Table 1.5 Brown 'odds-on' for the Labour leadership

Such end-of-year odds, however, were not representative of the previous 11 months, as 2006 was a year of ups and downs for the chancellor. For example, just a few weeks earlier, on 10 September, a headline in the *Observer* read 'Cabinet turns on Brown in a hunt for "alternative PM"'. Indeed, the failed 'September coup' and the way in which the chancellor had handled the situation had, it was argued, shown him in a less than favourable light. By that stage, few were arguing in favour of the kind of 'coronation' that had once appeared inevitable, with two-thirds of respondents in an ICM poll for the *Guardian* in early September wanting a genuine contest to choose the next premier. By 11 September, even Gordon Brown was briefing the press to the effect that he, too, would prefer a real contest rather than a clear run at the leadership. With so-called Blairite 'outriders' such as Byers and Milburn briefing against the chancellor, it appeared that a genuine contest might indeed be in the offing.

The problem is that candidates of the calibre necessary to give the chancellor a real test are few and far between. Even those who were advanced by Brown's critics inside cabinet (see Box 1.4) were poorly placed to capitalise on the chancellor's difficulties in the second half of the year, as is made evident below.

Box 1.4 A heavyweight challenge to Brown

'A cabinet source said that while they had not settled on a rival candidate yet, the events of the week had now tipped the balance decisively in favour of a genuine contest involving someone of "credibility and stature" standing against Brown. Alan Johnson, Alan Milburn, John Reid and Charles Clarke are potential names.'

Source: adapted from Gaby Hinsliff and Ned Temko, 'Cabinet turns on Brown in hunt for "alternative MP"', *Observer*, 10 September 2006.

Charles Clarke

Clarke had left the cabinet under a cloud following the debacle over the release of foreign prisoners. His vitriolic attack on the chancellor on 8 September — in which he described Brown's grinning when leaving Downing Street at the height of the crisis as 'absolutely stupid' — did as much damage to his own chances of a quick return to the front benches as it did to Brown's prospects of becoming leader.

Alan Milburn

Milburn was also out of the cabinet, having returned briefly to help organise the party's 2005 general election campaign. He was said to have briefed against Brown on Blair's behalf but did not appear to have the base from which to launch a leadership challenge of his own.

John Reid

Having widely been seen as a 'fixer' who could be sent in to sort out government departments, John Reid appeared to have met his match in the Home Office — a department that, by his own admission, was 'not fit for purpose'. The odds that were on offer on 9 November (see Table 1.5) would certainly add weight to the view that Reid's time at the Home Office had not been an unreserved success, despite his good showing at the party conference in September, when many had regarded him as a serious challenger for the leadership.

Alan Johnson

Widely seen as a 'safe pair of hands', the education secretary had quickly become established as a serious candidate for the post of deputy leader following Prescott's earlier difficulties. Some felt that he might even have the potential to challenge for the post of party leader. However, the results of ICM research for the *Guardian*, using an online panel, gave a more modest view of Johnson's potential (see Box 1.5).

Notwithstanding the problems of having a post-devolution party leader at Westminster who is returned from a Scottish constituency (see Chapter 9), it appeared by the end of November 2006 that Brown was the only realistic contender for the post of Labour leader. This reality meant that the media became more focused on the race to become deputy leader, for which there was an increasingly large and varied field.

As well as those already identified as possible challengers in the leadership contest (see Box 1.4), others such as David Miliband (seen by many as the next Labour leader but one), Hilary Benn, John Hutton, Peter Hain and Jack Straw were also expected to enter the race to succeed Prescott as deputy leader. For Patrick Wintour of the *Guardian*, Hain's ability to carry the support of the unions with his centre-left politics gave him the edge over many of his potential rivals. Harriet Harman, who in May had argued that 'an all-male team will never deliver for women', was also seen as a serious candidate by some observers.

Will a change in leader mean a change in direction for the government?

Blair's admission that the 2006 Party Conference would be his last as leader prompted renewed speculation regarding the future direction of the party. For some party elders, such as Michael Meacher, Blair's departure offered a potential 'springboard for a democratic renewal'. In an article in the *Guardian* on 3 August, the former Labour environment minister argued that 'a new cross-party convention should be established to draw up a blueprint to present to the people of this country for their approval'. Meacher was not alone in making such a call to arms. Others on the left had also started to prepare the ground for the post-Blair era (see Box 1.6).

In view of the fact that this post-Blair era is likely to be presided over by Brown, it was hardly surprising that by the end of 2006 commentators were starting to ask questions about the chancellor's own political creed. Though Blair's advisers were said to be trying to tie his successor to a 10-year strategy that would ensure their own man's political legacy, Brown appeared loath to buy into Blair's vision of the next decade — a reluctance that contributed in no small part to the September stand-off. By the time of the Labour party conference, however, the chancellor was clearly looking to set out his own vision.

Although it was considered likely that Brown would pursue many of the policies developed under Blair, it was suggested that the blueprint for a Brown premiership might be different in a number of key respects:

- There would be greater emphasis on the notion of 'Britishness' and a more concerted effort in respect of enhancing social cohesion.
- There might be an increased willingness to address — as opposed to simply talk about — climate change and other global challenges such as that posed by poverty and endemic disease in the developing world.
- Where possible, power would be devolved away from the centre as a means of giving communities more autonomy.
- It might prove desirable to codify and entrench properly the UK constitution.

In short, what Brown appeared to be offering was a 'softer' form of Blairism, accompanied by a desire to re-engage with voters and thereby win back their trust. Brown aimed to build on the economic stability that he had worked to create as chancellor, while pursuing policies rooted more firmly in his own social conscience. Such themes were well to the fore in the chancellor's speech at the 2006 Labour Party Conference (see Box 1.7).

Box 1.7 The Brown vision

'The "good society" theme of Gordon Brown's speech echoed the title of a book by the influential Canadian-American economist J. K. Galbraith. In *The Good Society: The Humane Agenda*, Galbraith argued for an equitable society that shows compassion for the poor while providing economic opportunity for all its citizens.

This was reflected in the choice of words for Mr Brown's speech yesterday: "people" was mentioned 43 times, and "community" or "communities" 25 times. Other buzzwords: society/social (16); citizen/citizenship (11); education (10); values (15); talent(s) (12); responsibility/responsibilities (13); change(s) (20); Britain/British (42); England/English (4); Scotland/Scottish (4); Tony (6); Tories (1).'

Source: adapted from Will Woodward and Larry Elliott, 'From Britishness to Blair: the Brown vision', *Guardian*, 26 September 2006.

Conclusion

Though issues of continuity and vision were vexing some groups in the parliamentary Labour Party by the end of 2006, any objective assessment of the lay of the land would have identified more immediate problems for the New Labour project. First, although Brown was the clear favourite to succeed Blair with the bookmakers, the broader public was far less convinced of his qualities. Polls taken throughout 2006 consistently showed that Labour would fare little better — and might perhaps even perform worse — with the chancellor at the helm than it would in the event that Blair held on until 2010. Indeed, it was said that private polling for the Labour Party had indicated that the chancellor was less popular in marginal constituencies than Blair and might, therefore, lose Labour the next election. Second, there was a widespread feeling that any Labour leadership election should be followed by a snap general election at which voters would have the opportunity to give the new leadership team their seal of approval. In a poll for ITV's *The Sunday Edition* in September, for example, 39% favoured a general election immediately after the election of a new Labour leader, and a further 17% called for a contest within 6 months. With the party trailing badly in the polls and the police investigation into the alleged sale of peerages yet to report, Brown could have been forgiven for envying David Miliband's unofficial role as the 'next Labour leader but one'.

Summary

- Tony Blair's decision to announce his intention not to seek a fourth term as party leader before the third term had even been won did more to fuel speculation over questions of timing and the succession than it did to end it.

- The prime minister's reluctance to set out a clear timetable, aggravated by a number of contextual factors, led to what some referred to as an attempted leadership coup at the start of September 2006.

- Though Blair survived this 'coup', the events of 1–7 September damaged the chancellor's standing. This setback — allied to poor poll ratings — saw Labour insiders looking for a credible alternative to Brown as next Labour leader.

- Public support for a Brown-led Labour Party, particularly among those voters in marginal constituencies, also seemed unimpressive.

- In November 2006, Brown remained the odds-on favourite to become the next Labour leader and prime minister. Media attention focused instead on the race to become his deputy.

- By the end of 2006, the chancellor was trying to set out a clear vision of what a Brown premiership might bring to the country.

Chapter 2

Cameron's Conservatives: on the road to recovery?

About this chapter

When David Cameron was elected leader of the Conservative Party at the end of 2005, he pledged to 'prioritise the pursuit of power'. But how much progress did he achieve during 2006? This chapter will assess the Cameron strategy and try to measure its impact by answering the following questions:

- Have Cameron's attempts to 'modernise' and 'liberalise' the Tories made them attractive to swing voters?
- Has he alienated the party's 'core' voters without securing enough new support to win a general election?
- What is the essence of Cameron's Conservatism?
- Is the new Tory leader effectively 'rebranding' his party, or is he (as one Conservative journalist remarked) 'all style and no substance'?

Cameron's challenge: an 'electoral Everest'?

David Cameron began 2006 by reminding his party of 'the electoral Everest that must be climbed' if it were to regain office. Addressing the Conservative Councillors' conference, he highlighted certain 'killer facts' that emerged from the 2005 general election:

- The Conservative Party had now suffered three heavy defeats in succession.
- It had failed again to win even a third of the votes cast.
- It had failed again to win even 200 seats.
- It polled even fewer votes in 2005 than in 1997.
- Its support among women and middle-class voters had failed again.
- Only 2% of its seats were outside England.
- It won no seats in Manchester, Liverpool, Leeds, Sheffield and Newcastle, where it was also outpolled by the Liberal Democrats.
- It needs to win a further 126 seats to gain a parliamentary majority — four times as many as it won in 2005.
- It needs a swing of 9% to gain the barest of seat majorities — almost twice the largest Tory swing ever recorded.
- The party had a huge image problem, which prevented it from advancing policies (on immigration, crime and Europe) that were, in themselves, popular (see Table 2.1).

With which party do you associate the following statements?	With the Conservatives	With Labour
'It appeals to one section of society rather than society as a whole.'	48%	20%
'It seems old-fashioned and stuck in the past.'	45%	11%
'It is extreme.'	41%	18%

Source: YouGov.

Table 2.1 Perceptions of the Conservative Party, May 2005

Cameron's prescription: the politics of apology?

For Cameron, addressing the 'image' problem outlined in Table 2.1 was fundamental: until this problem was overcome, it would be impossible to communicate individual Tory policies. Phrases such as 'decontamination', 'clearing the airwaves' and 'rebranding' thus became synonymous with the new Tory leader and his closest advisers (see Table 2.2). In other words, like Blair and New Labour 10 years earlier, Cameron sought to distance his party from its most recent past and effectively apologise for its previous conduct.

Name	Age	Position
George Osborne	35	Shadow chancellor
Edward Llewellyn	39	Chief of staff
George Bridges	37	Head of campaigns
George Eustace	35	Head of press
Steve Hilton	39	Director of communications
Danny Kruger	31	Chief speechwriter
Desmond Swayne	50	Leader's Private Parliamentary Secretary (PPS)
Oliver Letwin	49	Head of policy
Nicholas Boles	40	Head of Policy Exchange think-tank

Table 2.2 Cameron's team: the Tory leader's inner circle, 2006

Built to Last: 'rebranding' explained

Cameron's 'rebranding' mission involved a simple objective: associating Conservatives once again with the middle ground of British politics. Put another way, Cameron aimed to make his party attractive to those who had voted Liberal Democrat or New Labour. This strategy marked a break with that of the last two general elections, when the party (having initially flirted with

'inclusive' policies) ended up trying to mobilise its core vote — stressing the importance of 'saving the pound' in 2001 and immigration plus tax cuts in 2005. The signal failure of this strategy made it easier for Cameron to launch, and stick with, his own centrist approach after 2005.

Cameron's centrism, which he liked to dub 'modern', 'compassionate' or 'liberal' Conservatism, was highlighted by the policy document *Built to Last*, released in August 2006. Though it is deliberately vague, it is possible to discern from it ten clear themes.

1 De-prioritising Europe

Although voters were scarcely Europhile, Cameron sensed that Euroscepticism made the party look insular, xenophobic and obsessive. As he told the 2006 Tory conference, 'While voters worried about public services, job security and mortgage repayments, we were banging on about Europe.' It must be added that Cameron was seeking to downgrade, rather than change, the party's Euroscepticism. Nevertheless, his plan to disengage Tory MEPs from the European People's Party (a transnational group of centre-right MEPs with federalist leanings) was shelved once it provoked fresh Tory divisions and unhelpful headlines in the press.

2 De-prioritising immigration

In a year when immigration and multiculturalism became vital issues, the Tories were almost silent on the subject, allowing ministers such as John Reid and Jack Straw to advance 'Conservative' analyses. Cameron, it seemed, had no wish to reinforce the party's association with its traditional concerns, sensing this would undermine his efforts to reinvent it. But he may have also reckoned that immigration will always be an issue on which voters think the Tories 'strong', irrespective of whether their leaders talk about it.

3 Prioritising public services

For two reasons, Cameron has tried to focus on public services such as health and education: first, to help the party look more mainstream and 'compas-sionate'; second, to reflect the concerns of voters in the party's own focus groups. This strategy, central to *Built to Last*'s agenda, led to a number of initiatives in 2006:

- *De-prioritising tax cuts*. Cameron feared that the party's interest in tax cuts would frighten voters into thinking a Tory government would slash public spending. Journalists were therefore told — repeatedly — that the party's priority was now 'economic stability' over lower taxation (thus refuting the old Thatcherite notion that lower tax was a *precondition* of economic stability). Though tax cuts were still held to be a long-term goal, Cameron made it clear that he would 'share the proceeds of growth' between tax cuts and higher spending on key public services. This represents a significant concession to the 'Brown settlement': since 1997, the overall tax burden has risen by 3%, while public spending has risen by about 6%

in relation to gross domestic product — a trend that Cameron seems happy to extend. In October, the leadership rejected *Tax Matters*, a party report on taxes chaired by Lord Forsyth, which recommended a £21 billion cut in taxation, and promised to 'rebalance' rather than reduce the overall tax burden.

- *Ditching of the 'Patients Passport'.* A 'flagship' policy in the 2005 manifesto, the Patients Passport policy (allowing patients to choose private treatment that the state would subsidise) was dropped in early 2006, for fear that it would signal only a lukewarm commitment to the NHS.
- *Ditching of grammar school expansion.* Anxious to be seen as a party that would 'improve education for all', Cameron let it be known that he did not support the traditional Tory goal of 'a grammar school in every town', claiming that this distracted from the issue of state education overall. He also indicated that he would educate his own children in the state sector.
- *'Three magic letters'.* Cameron underlined his commitment to public services by claiming that three letters — 'N.H.S.' — summarised his very purpose in politics. With reference to the disability of his eldest child, he duly reminded delegates of his family's 'vested interest' in the health service, promising to match — and even outstrip — Labour's increased spending on the NHS.

4 Acknowledging some New Labour reforms

Another clear pitch for the centre ground was Cameron's concession that 'not all Labour's reforms have been wrong', citing in particular the minimum wage, the Bank of England's power to set interest rates, the 'New Deal' job-training programme, the 'Sure Start' pre-school education scheme and devolution for Scotland and Wales (thus shelving the 2005 policy of allowing Welsh voters a referendum on closing the Welsh Assembly).

5 Interest in poverty

The party's deference to Gordon Brown was reflected in its pledge to combat poverty. The advice of Sir Bob Geldof was also sought, with two of Cameron's six specialist policy groups addressing the issue (see Table 2.3).

Policy group	Chair
Social Justice	Iain Duncan Smith
Quality of Life	John Gummer
Globalisation and Global Poverty	Peter Lilley
Public Services	Stephen Dorrell
National and International Security	Pauline Neville-Jones
Economic Competitiveness	John Redwood

Table 2.3 Tory Policy Commissions, 2006

6 Environmentalism

The slogan 'Vote Blue, Go Green' formed the bedrock of the Tory campaign in the 2006 local elections, with Cameron emphasising his links with environmental expert Zac Goldsmith. In the context of global warming, Cameron said that he would 'stand up to, and not just for, business' and promised 'binding annual targets' for reducing carbon emissions. In October, Shadow Chancellor George Osborne hinted at further 'green taxes' on cars, petrol and short-haul air flights.

7 Acknowledgement of 'alternative' family structures

Cameron surprised many at the 2006 Tory conference by claiming that 'relationships involving long-term commitment' were not confined to heterosexual marriages. Implicitly endorsing Labour's Civil Partnership Act 2004, he declared that 'marriage means something whether you're a man and a woman, a woman and a woman, or a man and a man'.

8 A more 'sociological' approach to law and order

Distancing himself from the traditional Tory assumption that crime was about individual lapses, Cameron paid homage to the liberal view that crime reflects social as well as individual failure. In a clear echo of Blairism, he argued that Tories must be tough not just on crime but also on its causes, implying that offenders were often the effects as well as causes of a dysfunctional culture (thus sparking the journalistic jibe that Cameron advocated 'hugging a hoodie').

9 Constitutional reform

Cameron's team claimed that 'modernisation' of the British constitution had been hijacked by the party's opponents and that it was time to 'reclaim' the party's interest in the subject. A 'Democracy Taskforce', chaired by former Tory chancellor Kenneth Clarke, recommended a largely elective House of Lords, a British bill of rights, a diminished number of MPs and new curbs on financial donations to political parties (see Chapter 5). It was also looking at ways to solve the 'West Lothian Question' (see Chapter 9) resulting from Scottish devolution, and did not rule out the idea that, at Westminster, MPs from English constituencies should vote on matters affecting only English voters.

10 Combating racism and sexism

Cameron echoed the Lib-Lab view that discrimination was often fuelled by the dearth of women and ethnic minority representatives in public life. A new 'A-list' of Tory candidates — 55% women, 10% black — was duly established in early 2006, designed to ensure that more female and ethnic minority candidates contested winnable Tory seats. The leadership feared that local party democracy was not always compatible with a more 'inclusive' range of candidates, so steps were taken to curb the powers of constituency associations in areas of candidate selection (see Box 2.1).

Selecting Tory candidates: rule changes, 2006

(i) Associations (constituency Tory parties) in target seats with fewer than 300 members will be expected to choose parliamentary candidates via American-style 'primary' ballots, where non-party members will be allowed to vote. This idea was pioneered by the Warrington S. and Reading E. associations before the 2005 general election.

(ii) In larger associations, the membership will choose a shortlist, half of whom must be women. The local executive will make the final selection. This arrangement reverses the previous procedure.

(iii) The selection of the Conservative candidate for the next London mayor election will be open to all voters in Greater London. A special selection panel will shortlist candidates, arrange hustings open to the public, and then allow London's voters to text, telephone and e-mail their preferences.

(iv) The local executive is encouraged to consider seriously, but not compelled to select, any applicant from the party's 'A-list'.

Built to Last: the ballot

To suppress claims that the party had been hijacked by a 'Notting Hill clique', Cameron held an all-party ballot on the *Built to Last* document during the summer of 2006. Ninety-three percent of the ballot papers returned endorsed its proposals.

Cameron's Conservatism: a break with the past?

Amid claims that Cameron has 'betrayed' the spirit of recent Conservative governments, it needs to be pointed out that, in several key areas, Cameron's policies show continuity with the Conservatism of the 1980s and 1990s:

- There is still an aspiration — albeit long term — to cut taxation. Unlike Labour, which believes that economic growth should fund only extra public spending, Cameron's Tories say the proceeds of growth should also reduce the tax burden.
- There is still a belief that privatisation should be extended.
- The leadership is still sceptical of EU integration. George Osborne reminded the 2006 Tory conference that the party would 'never' join the single currency, while Cameron hinted that it would renegotiate the UK's whole relationship with the EU. This persistent Euroscepticism was also inherent to Cameron's plan for a British bill of rights, replacing the Human Rights Act 1998, itself based on the European Charter of Human Rights.
- This more subtle Euroscepticism linked up with a more subtle, lingering interest in immigration. Cameron has called for a review of the UK's border controls — largely determined at present by EU rulings.
- Although Cameron defined it more 'inclusively', there is still a firm belief in marriage and the family. As Cameron told the 2006 party conference, 'family

instability is the root of almost every social problem'. Osborne has supported the restoration of the married couples allowance, abolished by Gordon Brown in 2000.

Cameron has fostered the impression — like Blair with Labour after 1994 — that the party had changed dramatically under his leadership. But this, too, is misleading. Cameron was a principal author of the 2005 Tory manifesto and, as Box 2.2 shows, it made consensual noises in a number of areas.

> **Box 2.2** **Precursors of 'Cameronism': some themes of the 2005 Tory manifesto**
>
> ■ A commitment to match Labour's proposed increases in public spending
> ■ An acceptance of the minimum wage
> ■ An acceptance of the winter fuel payment to pensioners
> ■ An acceptance of the raised National Insurance payments
> ■ No plans to raise the threshold for higher rate of income tax (Labour's failure to do so after 1997 had doubled the number of people paying it)
> ■ A mere £4 billion of tax cuts (described as 'chicken-feed' by the free-market think-tank, Adam Smith Institute)

The politics of Cameron: pre-Thatcherite Conservatism?

One interesting theory about Cameron's agenda is that it is a 'throwback' to a much earlier form of Conservatism that became marginalised during the Thatcher era. This was the 'one-nation Conservatism' associated with Disraeli, Baldwin, Macmillan, Eden and Home. Cameron has echoed this ancestral Conservatism in a number of ways:

- *A stress on community*. Cameron's call for a more 'together' society and an end to 'me-ism' updates his party's rejection of liberalism in the nineteenth century, which it associated with irresponsible individualism.
- *Concerns about poverty*. Disraeli's coining of the phrase 'One Nation' came from his belief that poverty must be addressed in the interests of social cohesion. Cameron's message to the 2006 Tory conference drew upon this strain in Tory thinking.
- *State intervention*. Following on from these concerns about poverty, Cameron's stress on public services reflects traditional Conservatism's rejection of the liberal/laissez-faire society. Some have argued that the welfare state is rooted in Disraeli's 'paternalistic' legislation of the 1870s (e.g. the Artisans' Dwellings Act 1875), and of course it should be remembered that postwar Conservatism abetted the expansion of the NHS and the welfare state.
- *Proto-environmentalism*. Cameron is not the first Tory leader to voice doubts about the effects of industrialisation. Disraeli expressed similar

concerns, while Stanley Baldwin (Tory leader 1923–37) wrote that 'the values of the countryside are the real values of England'.

- *Paternalistic leadership*. Until the mid-1960s, the Tories were characterised by aristocratic, public-school leaders with a patrician concern for the social fabric. Cameron is the first Tory leader since Alec Douglas-Home (1963–65) to be educated at public school, and it has not gone unnoticed that his 'inner circle' (see Table 2.2) is packed with fellow old Etonians and products of exclusive schools (Letwin, Llewellyn, Eustace, Bridges and Kruger all went to Eton, while George Osborne was educated at St Paul's. This gave rise to claims that Cameron has led a public-school putsch inside the party, restoring its traditional character after decades of 'meritocratic' leadership.

Perhaps the difference between Cameron's Conservatism and that of his predecessors is the same as that between the born-into-wealth, public-school upper class and the upwardly mobile, grammar-school middle class: whereas the former felt secure enough to stress altruistic concerns about social responsibility, the latter — reflecting their own careers — tended to stress individual responsibility, enterprise and freedom.

Why has there been this apparent restoration of the *ancien régime*? One possible explanation is that, after the end of the Cold War, the *embourgeoisement* of Labour and the debacle of the Major government, the party became less attractive to the aspirant middle class and more reliant upon its traditional source of politicians. It is ironic that calls for the party to reach beyond its core-vote support are now coming from its core-source representatives.

Has Cameron made a difference?

There are two ways of answering this question: first in relation to party members and second in relation to voters.

Party members: unreconstructed?

It may be the case that, while party members' instincts are unchanged, these instincts have been tempered since 2005 by an awareness of past mistakes and a new thirst for power — a trend embodied by Cameron's emergence as leader, and then quickened by the style of his leadership. As Box 2.3 reveals, there is substantial support among Tory members for Cameron's centrist policies.

Box 2.3	**Which policies should the Conservative Party pursue? The views of Tory members**

It should commit itself to running public services pretty much along the same lines as now, spend as much money on them as efficiency requires, while trying to limit taxation by cutting out bureaucracy and waste. *Agree: 55%*

It should drastically reduce the role of the state by introducing large tax cuts, by reducing the number of bureaucrats and by extending privatisation. *Agree: 34%*

Source: YouGov, October 2006.

However, there are limits to Cameron's support inside the party. It should be noted, for example, that in the *Built to Last* ballot, only 27% of eligible members voted — so only approximately a quarter have given clear support to Cameron's agenda.

The letters page of the *Daily Telegraph*, always a good barometer of grass-roots Tory opinion, revealed further intra-Tory doubts about the Cameron project (see Box 2.4). These comments imply no small amount of sympathy for the sort of views expressed by Tory dissenters such as journalist Simon Heffer, who has claimed repeatedly that Cameron's Toryism is 'all spin and no substance', and former party chairman Lord Tebbit, who complained that 'the party is aping Blair at precisely the moment when Blairism is discredited'.

Box 2.4	Dissenting voices: a selection of letters to the *Daily Telegraph*, October 2006

'David Cameron has ignored the issues uppermost in the minds of voters: crime, policing, education, council tax and immigration. The Government has failed miserably in these areas, but all we hear from the Tories are banalities.'

'I have always voted for the Conservative Party, but after Mr Cameron's speech [to the Tory conference] there is no longer the option to do so. The choice is now between New Labour and newer Labour.'

'Before making his speech, Mr Cameron ought to have donned a black cap, pronouncing the death of the Conservative Party.'

'I was thinking of visiting Mr Cameron at Westminster. I wonder if there's anything he'd like me to bring him from planet Earth.'

For Tebbit and Heffer, the key task is to regain support from the swathe of middle-class voters who abstained at the last two general elections. This can be achieved, they argue, by stressing bedrock Tory themes such as tax and immigration, but with more conviction and polish than in 2001 and 2005.

Candidate selection also suggests that the reform of party attitudes only goes so far. The impact of Cameron's 'A-list' (see pp. 18–19) — designed to give the party a more inclusive and metropolitan look in a general election — has not been huge, largely because local party members are still not compelled to choose from it (see Box 2.1).

In some cases, the local party has simply refused to select A-listed candidates — as for the Bromley and Chislehurst by-election, where activists chose local businessman Bob Neill. Even when shortlists did include 'listers', local members often frustrated national officials by not choosing women or black candidates. Folkestone and Hythe, for example, chose Damien Collins ahead of two A-listed women, despite 'not so subtle recommendations by Conservative Central Office' (*Daily Telegraph*, 5 August). By October, only

31% of candidates selected for safe Tory seats were women — a smaller percentage than between 2001 and 2005.

It seems fair to conclude that the party's support for 'Cameronism' is highly contingent upon electoral success. If this is not attained, Cameron could be pressured — as his three predecessors were — into a more conventional form of Tory politics.

Voters: confused and unsure?

During 2006, the party's progress at the polls was mixed. In the May local elections, it did have some cause for jubilation:

- It won almost 40% of votes cast, its best performance in any nationwide elections since 1992, and 13% more votes than Labour — the sort of figures that would give an overall Tory majority at the next general election.
- It gained control of 15 local authorities. That these included Bassetlaw, Chorley and Coventry suggested that the party was at last making progress beyond its southern heartlands.

However, in most respects, the 2006 elections showed that the Conservative party still had far to travel:

- In the local elections, the party made virtually no progress in northern metropolitan areas and still have no councillors in Manchester, Liverpool and Newcastle.
- Its vote share in the local elections was not much higher than in 2000 and 2004, a year before it crashed to defeat in a general election.
- Its performance in two of the three parliamentary by-elections was dismal — gaining just 8% of votes in Dunfermline and West Fife and under 4% in Blaenau Gwent. Although these were never seats that the Tories could win, a party on course for power should not be doing this badly in any part of the country.
- Its performance in the Bromley and Chislehurst by-election also caused alarm: its majority fell from over 13 000 at the general election to just 633. If the Tories are struggling to win their own seats, their chances of gaining those of other parties do not look good. For those on the Tory right, the result fed fears that current policies were alienating core voters while not impressing those on the centre-left.
- Its performance in the mayoral elections was also poor, failing to gain a quarter of first-preference votes in any of the four contests (see Chapter 4).

YouGov opinion polls in the autumn confirmed that the party under Cameron had improved its ratings by an average of 6%, but that it was now flat-lining on 38% and leading Labour by just 4–6% — not enough, given the vagaries of the electoral system, to win power at a general election. It is worth recalling that when the Conservative Party was last on course for power — under Heath in the late 1960s and Thatcher in the late 1970s — it was sometimes 20% clear of Labour.

Why are voters still cagey?

According to YouGov (see Table 2.4), voters acknowledge that Cameron is trying to change his party and seem unconcerned by his privileged background. Yet they still have reservations stemming from four factors:

- They are unsure what the Tories now stand for. As such…
- …they are unconvinced that the party as a whole has changed.
- They are unconvinced that the Tories, compared with Labour, occupy the middle ground (where two-thirds of voters claim to be).
- They doubt the party's commitment to the public services.

1. Under David Cameron, the Conservatives have acquired a new vitality.
Agree: 47%
2. David Cameron is a 'toff', remote from ordinary people.
Agree: 25%
3. Despite Cameron's youth, the Conservatives still seem an old-fashioned party.
Agree: 40%
4. It is hard to know what a Conservative government under David Cameron would be like.
Agree: 58%
5. Cameron 'talks a good game', but it is hard to know if there is any substance behind the words.
Agree: 60%
6. The Conservatives still cannot be trusted to run public services.
Agree: 42%
7. How far from the centre is David Cameron?
Average response: 34 points to the right
8. How far from the centre is the Conservative Party?
Average response: 50 points to the right
9. How far from the centre is the Labour Party?
Average response: 19 points to the left

Source: YouGov, October 2006.

Table 2.4 Public perceptions of the Tory Party, October 2006

Conclusion: jury still out?

It seems fair to argue that Cameron is the party's most influential leader for a decade, and for two reasons:

- He has persuaded large sections of the party to change.
- He has made some voters think afresh about the Conservative Party.

However, Cameron would be the first to acknowledge that his party's battle to save itself has only just begun; a fear corroborated by the elections and opinion polls of 2006. If further, more substantial, progress is to be made, he will need to juggle five objectives in the years ahead:

- continue projecting the centrist message demanded by most 'swing' voters
- avoid alienating the party's core electorate, which UKIP (now under new leadership) is intent on wooing
- resist any reactionary pressures inside his own party
- dispel the charge that he is 'all style' by developing specific, substantive policies that will enthuse both the party and the electorate
- respond effectively to a new Labour leader and, perhaps, a rejuvenated Labour government

Summary

- Cameron has tried to relocate the Conservative Party in the political centre.
- He has launched some eye-catching ideas to attract Lib-Lab voters.
- He has tried to sideline the party's Thatcherite wing.
- He has had limited success in influencing the selection of candidates.
- He has been cautious about enunciating specific policies.
- He remains vulnerable to the criticism of 'all spin and no substance'.
- Voters are less hostile to, but still sceptical of, Cameron's Tory party.

Chapter 3

The Liberal Democrats: is there life after Charlie?

About this chapter

2006 was a turbulent year for the UK's third party. The controversial resignation of the Liberal Democrat leader was followed by an equally controversial leadership contest. This chapter will answer the following questions:

- Why was Charles Kennedy forced to resign?
- Did the leadership contest make the party a 'laughing stock' or was it 'a triumph for party democracy'?
- Why did Sir Menzies Campbell win?
- Will the Liberal Democrats under Campbell 'talk left but walk right'?
- What are the prospects for the party under Campbell?
- Is Campbell a 'stopgap leader'?

The 2006 leadership battle: a necessary contest?

Within the first week of 2006, the Liberal Democrats were locked into a battle for the leadership — and therefore the future direction — of their party. Yet just 6 months earlier, at the 2005 general election, they had achieved the highest number of third-party MPs since the 1920s. So why did Charles Kennedy, the leader who helped achieve this feat, find his position under fire at the start of 2006?

Charles Kennedy: at fault in the general election?

Despite the increased number of Liberal Democrat seats (a net gain of 11), the general feeling inside the party after the 2005 general election was that it should have done better — especially given the unpopularity of the government and the unimpressive state of the Conservative Party. For many Liberal Democrat MPs, the blame for their limited progress rested with the leader and his alleged fondness for (what one MP termed) 'more than a wee dram'. According to those MPs, this led to a number of problems at the 2005 general election, for example:

- the launch of the Liberal Democrat manifesto was an almost farcical affair, with the leader slurring his words and failing to explain the party's tax policies clearly
- the style of the leader's campaign was too relaxed and languid; with party politics in a state of flux, and with unique opportunities for 'alternative' parties to win votes, a more dynamic and crusading form of leadership was required

Nonetheless, Kennedy remained a popular figure with voters and in January 2006 there was still no obvious candidate to succeed him.

Why did criticism of Kennedy intensify?

At the very beginning of 2006, Kennedy faced renewed criticism from inside his party, involving the following charges:

- He had failed to develop any clear strategy for dealing with Cameron's Conservatives. As Lord McNally, the Liberal Democrat leader in the House of Lords, remarked: 'Charles has failed to make the radical, rapid and sustained change of style and content needed in the new political climate.'
- He was allegedly drunk at a number of Liberal Democrat shadow cabinet meetings.
- He had failed to turn up at a Christmas party rally in Newcastle, citing 'family reasons'.
- His fellow MPs were said to be tired of 'covering up' for their leader's personal problems.

By 4 January, ITN learned that 11 of Kennedy's most senior colleagues had sent him a letter (see Tables 3.1 and 3.2), urging resignation. Pre-empting ITN's 'scoop', Kennedy convened a press conference on 5 January, admitting to both alcoholism and the unease of his colleagues. But instead of resigning, as most of his shadow cabinet probably hoped, Kennedy announced that he would trigger a leadership contest, inviting all party members to reaffirm his leadership. This audacious move quickly backfired. Sarah Teather, Edward Davey and more than 20 other senior MPs said that they could no longer support Kennedy's leadership, while Chris Davies (leader of the party's MEPs) described him as a 'dead man walking'. The result was that, though Kennedy's planned leadership contest would proceed, it was not one that would involve Kennedy himself: he resigned the following day.

Date	Event
30 November 2005	Ten Lib Dem MPs urge Menzies Campbell to write letter of 'no confidence' to Kennedy
13 December	Revolt against Kennedy in Lib Dem shadow cabinet meeting
15 December	Vincent Cable organises letter of 'no confidence', signed by himself and ten other front-benchers
4 January 2006	ITN warns Kennedy it will break the story about his alcoholism
5 January	Kennedy calls press conference: admits to alcoholism and instigates leadership contest
6 January	Twenty-five Lib Dem spokespeople threaten to resign unless Kennedy quits
7 January	Kennedy resigns

Table 3.1 Countdown to resignation: the fall of Charles Kennedy

Name	Position
Norman Baker	Shadow environment secretary
Vincent Cable	Shadow chancellor
Edward Davey	Shadow education and skills secretary
Andrew George	Shadow international development secretary
Sandra Gidley	Shadow minister for women and pensioners
Chris Huhne	Shadow chief secretary to the Treasury
Norman Lamb	Shadow trade and industry secretary
David Laws	Shadow secretary for work and pensions
Michael Moore	Shadow defence secretary
Sarah Teather	Shadow secretary for community and local government
John Thurso	Shadow Scottish secretary

Table 3.2 The assassins — signatories of the no-confidence letter on 15 December 2005

The 2006 leadership contest: a credit to the party?

Following Kennedy's departure, there were, initially, four candidates to succeed him:

- *Sir Menzies Campbell*. Deputy party leader and foreign affairs spokesman, he was seen as a mainstream Liberal Democrat, palatable to all sections of the party.
- *Simon Hughes*. Legal affairs spokesman and Liberal Democrat president, he was linked to the left of the party and was keen on tackling poverty and urban deprivation through higher tax and public spending. He was a favoured candidate among the party's activists in Labour-held northern seats.
- *Mark Oaten*. Home affairs spokesman and co-author of the party's contentious *Orange Book* (commending lower tax and a more market-friendly approach), he was feared by Cameron's Tories but had limited support from Liberal Democrat members.
- *Chris Huhne*. Treasury spokesman, he was a late entrant to the contest and the least-known candidate. He was sympathetic to *Orange Book* economics, but fervently interested in environmental issues.

As the campaign began, the *Daily Telegraph* remarked: 'It looks set to be the dullest party leadership campaign…since the last Lib Dem leadership campaign.' Yet this view had to be revised after developments concerning two of the candidates — developments that prompted *The Times* to comment: 'Just as they were being accepted as a grown-up party, the Lib Dems have become a laughing stock once again.' These developments were:

- Revelations from a male prostitute about the sexual tastes of Mark Oaten, details of which were considered 'too disgusting to publish' by the *News of the World*. Oaten promptly withdrew from the contest.

- Revelations from Simon Hughes (prompted by tabloid rumours) that he had a homosexual past — despite winning his seat in 1982 with a by-election campaign that disparaged a homosexual Labour candidate. There were rumours that Hughes would also resign from the contest, but he persevered. However, there is little doubt that the episode damaged his prospects: having once been a serious contender, he eventually failed to come even second (see Table 3.3).

The Hughes and Oaten debacles strengthened the cause of Menzies Campbell. With the Liberal Democrats' previous leader damaged by drink, and two potential leaders damaged by sex, the party's desire for 'colourful' figures receded. Although Chris Huhne's campaign gained momentum, the party now seemed to want a 'safe pair of hands'. Campbell's victory was thus expected, though Huhne's support was impressive given his low profile at the campaign's outset.

	Candidate	Number of votes	Percentage of votes
First count	M. Campbell	23264	45%
	C. Huhne	16691	32%
	S. Hughes	12081	23%
	Hughes eliminated		
Second count	M. Campbell	29697	58%
	C. Huhne	21628	42%

Turnout: 72%

Note: Voting was conducted according to the supplementary vote system.

Table 3.3 The Lib Dem leadership contest 2006: the result

With 52036 party members participating, Liberal Democrat officials hailed the contest 'a triumph for party democracy'. But this was not strictly true. Kennedy was ousted, after all, by a *coup* of party MPs. If his fate had rested with the party as a whole, he might well have survived.

Date	Event
9 January	Nominations open
10–13 January	Menzies Campbell, Simon Hughes, Chris Huhne and Mark Oaten declare candidatures
19 January	Mark Oaten withdraws after lurid revelations
22 January	Simon Hughes discloses details of his sexuality
6 February	Ballot papers sent out to 72062 party members
2 March	Ballot papers counted and result announced
3 March	Winner acclaimed at Lib Dem Spring Conference in Harrogate

Table 3.4 The Liberal Democrat leadership contest 2006: a chronology

Campbell's 'route map': a leftward course?

Shortly after his election, Sir Menzies Campbell released what he called a 'route map' for the party under his leadership — one, he said, that would 'bind our party together and reflect all its concerns'. But what were its concerns? Campbell might well have been guided by an extensive survey of Liberal Democrat members, carried out by YouGov during the leadership campaign (see Table 3.5).

1. What should be the priorities of the new leader?				
Protecting civil liberties 63%	Combating climate change 54%	Reducing poverty 48%	Devolving power 36%	Electoral reform 34%
2. How serious a challenge to the party are Cameron's Tories?				
Serious 68%	Not serious 30%			
3. If there was no Lib Dem candidate in your constituency, how would you vote?				
Conservative 12%	Labour 24%	Another party 36%	Wouldn't vote 13%	
4. Where should the Lib Dems position themselves?				
Left of Labour 32%	Closer to Labour than the Tories 13%	Closer to the Tories than Labour 6%	Equidistant between the two main parties 38%	

Source: YouGov, 14 February 2006.

Table 3.5 The views of Liberal Democrat members, February 2006

YouGov's findings show that, although the Liberal Democrats recognised the threat of the resurgent Tories, their radical, centre-left instincts were still intact: 45% thought that the party should be close to, or even to the left of, Labour in its policies. It was also notable that, although 23% of Lib Dem voters in 2005 would have voted Tory if there had been no Liberal Democrat candidate available (YouGov, April 2005), the figure among Liberal Democrat members in February 2006 was just 12%.

In short, there was only limited support for the centre-right policies of the *Orange Book* authors. Indeed, a number of Liberal Democrat activists told the *Guardian* (12 January 2006) that, with Cameron leading the Tories, the Liberal Democrat party should now 'write off' further progress in southern England and explicitly target Labour voters in northern, working-class areas — a view strengthened by the party's success at the Dunfermline and West Fife by-election (see below).

Campbell was reluctant to embrace fully such a strategy, noting perhaps that there was strong support in the party for the 'equidistance' approach favoured by Kennedy. However, by the time he delivered his speech to the party conference in September, there were clear signs of him pushing the party in a leftward direction:

- Campbell explicitly described himself as 'centre-left' (a label that Kennedy avoided, preferring 'limitless appeal').
- He repeatedly denounced the 'right' (e.g. Thatcherites and neo-Conservatives) without expressing similar scorn for the 'left' (e.g. old Labour).
- He advocated a 'redistribution of wealth and power' — a phrase lifted straight from the socialist vocabulary.
- He advocated 'a crusade against poverty'.
- He promised £8 billion of new 'green taxes', including big increases in car tax for certain 'wealthy owner' vehicles (e.g. 'people carriers').

As the *Daily Telegraph* (29 September) bemoaned, 'The Lib Dems have taken a decisive shift to the left...their tax package will leave 2 million people up to £2 500 a year worse off. The measures make grim reading for middle England.'

Does Campbell have a hidden agenda?

Despite these leftist steps, columnists such as the *Guardian*'s Polly Toynbee believe that Campbell will 'talk left but walk right'. To support this claim, the following points are cited:
- his determination to drop the policy of a 50% tax rate for higher earners
- his support for the part-privatisation of the Royal Mail
- his lack of enthusiasm for the 2005 policy of scrapping council tax
- his promotion of *Orange Book*-ers (notably Vincent Cable, David Laws and Norman Lamb) to key positions in his shadow cabinet (see Table 3.6)
- rumours of a Lib-Con coalition in the (very likely) event of a hung parliament. In the words of one Liberal Democrat insider: 'Ming is very reluctant to prop up a Labour government that has lost its majority at Westminster, and thus the support of the country...given the centrist steps taken by Cameron, Ming thinks a deal with the Tories is more likely now than at any time since 1974' (*Guardian*, 15 September).

What did voters think?

The Liberal Democrats' future will be decided not just by themselves, but by voters. And, in a year when some predicted meltdown for a party rocked at national level, their overall performance in the 2006 elections was not disastrous (see Chapter 4).

It is true that there was some panic in Liberal Democrat ranks after the May local elections, in which little progress was made (momentum matters for third parties) and they lost council control in Islington and Milton Keynes. However, the party fared well in other elections, which showed that, post-Kennedy, the party was still a reputable force:
- At the Dunfermline and West Fife by-election, the Liberal Democrats won a hitherto safe Labour seat. The fact that it occurred during their scandal-strewn leadership contest made the victory all the more remarkable.

Name	Position
Paul Burstow	Chief whip
Vincent Cable	Shadow chancellor and deputy leader
Alistair Carmichael	Shadow transport secretary
Nick Clegg	Shadow home secretary
Edward Davey	Shadow trade and industry secretary
Don Foster	Shadow culture, media and sport secretary
Julia Goldsworthy	Shadow Treasury secretary
Nick Harvey	Shadow defence secretary
David Heath	Shadow leader of the House of Commons
Simon Hughes	Constitutional affairs and shadow attorney general
Chris Huhne	Shadow environment secretary
Susan Kramer	Shadow international development secretary
Norman Lamb	Leader's chief of staff
David Laws	Shadow secretary for work and pensions
Tom McNally	Leader in the House of Lords
Michael Moore	Shadow foreign secretary
Lembit Opik	Shadow Wales and Northern Ireland secretary
Andrew Stunnell	Shadow secretary for local government and communities
Jo Swinson	Shadow Scottish secretary
Matthew Taylor	Shadow secretary for social exclusion
Sarah Teather	Shadow education and skills secretary
Steve Webb	Shadow health secretary

Table 3.6 Campbell's shadow cabinet

- In the Bromley and Chislehurst by-election, they almost overturned a 13 000 Tory majority, thus proving that they were still a threat to Conservatives in the Cameron era.
- In the May elections, they still polled 25% of the votes and gained control of South Lakeland, St Albans and Richmond-upon-Thames, the latter being especially important as it was again at the expense of a supposedly resurgent Tory party.
- In the mayoral elections, Watford's Liberal Democrat incumbent secured re-election, while in Lewisham the party's candidate overtook the Tories into second place.

In summary, the party kept its head above water in one of its most troubled years. In the process, it proved that it was no 'top-down' party, dependent on dynamic national leadership — a reality that will have chastened both its Labour and Tory opponents.

However, the party's electoral prospects were not helped by the arrest of one of its most important supporters, businessman Michael Brown. Brown effectively financed the Liberal Democrat election campaign in 2005 and was jailed in September 2006 for fraud and deception. As a result, the party may have to repay Brown's £2 million worth of donations and find alternative donors for future elections. For a party that is already short of money, this would be a serious setback (see Chapter 5).

Conclusion: is Ming a stopgap leader?

Following Campbell's election as leader, some commentators argued that his task was to 'stop the rot' following the setbacks of 2005 and Kennedy's fall from grace; it would then be up to his successor to resume progress in the next parliament. By the end of 2006, this view needed serious revision. Given their performance at the 2006 elections, and Campbell's clear pitch for the centre-left vote, it is not implausible that the Liberal Democrats, as well as the Tories, will benefit from a collapse in Labour support at the next general election — particularly in Scotland and northern England, where Cameron's impact is yet to be felt.

We must also remember that opinion polls in 2006 point not to a Tory victory but to a hung parliament — the unspoken 'promised land' for Liberal Democrats. The party's role in such an outcome would be pivotal and could lead to participation in government. Though often derided as 'dull' and 'too old', Campbell might yet be the first Liberal leader in a cabinet since 1945.

Summary

- Kennedy's controversial departure left some bitterness among the Liberal Democrats — especially at grass-roots level.
- The ensuing leadership contest neither enhanced nor diminished the party's reputation.
- Despite a difficult year, the party remains a serious contender in UK elections.
- Campbell's rhetoric is centre-left, though many detect a discreet, centre-right agenda.
- The new leader's role could extend — and increase — beyond this parliament.

Chapter 4

Britain at the polls, 2006: what is the party system?

About this chapter

The 2005 general election did little to clarify the true nature of the UK's party system. Was it still a two-party system? Had a new party system emerged? If so, how could it be categorised? In 2006, there were a number of elections that renewed the debate. This chapter focuses on these elections and will answer the following questions:

- Is the UK's two-party system revived?
- Is the popularity of the Liberal Democrats now so great that the UK has an affirmed three-party system?
- Is Labour in a position to rule for many years to come, creating a dominant party system?
- Is the popularity of small parties and independents growing so fast that the UK now has a multi-party system?

Which elections took place in 2006?

For students of the UK party system, the key elections in 2006 were (in chronological order):

- the parliamentary by-election in Dunfermline and West Fife
- the English council elections
- the mayoral elections in Watford, Hackney, Lewisham and Newham
- the parliamentary and Welsh Assembly by-elections in Blaenau Gwent
- the parliamentary by-election in Bromley and Chislehurst

After the general election of 2005, there were numerous suggestions of which type of party system the UK had. The most challenging of these interpretations were as follows:

- *A revived two-party system.* A view advanced by Fraser Nelson in the *Spectator*, arguing that the Conservatives were again ready to mount a serious bid for power and that they were the only realistic alternative to Labour.
- *An affirmed three-party system.* A view advanced by Steve Richards in the *New Statesman*, arguing that the Liberal Democrats were a permanent, vital force in UK politics, and that there were two major oppositions to Labour.
- *A dominant party system.* A view advanced by Jackie Ashley in the *Guardian*, arguing that Labour alone was able to govern outright and was poised to emulate the long period of Tory rule after 1979.

- *A multi-party system.* A view advanced by Professor Vernon Bogdanor in the *Independent*, arguing that several parties were growing steadily following the collapse of Labour-Tory dominance.

In this chapter, we will assess these theories in view of elections held in 2006. In respect of the mayoral elections, we will also revisit the debate about alternative electoral systems.

The Dunfermline and West Fife by-election: the Liberal Democrats reborn?

The by-election in this Scottish constituency was held on 9 February, following the death of Labour MP Rachel Squire. Though it was held at a time of government unpopularity, Labour was confident of holding the seat, for four reasons:
- Dunfermline and West Fife was a solidly working-class constituency, which had returned Labour MPs since 1918.
- Even in 2005, when Labour's national vote share shrank by 5%, its majority in the constituency was 11500.
- The second-placed party in 2005, the Liberal Democrats, was in the middle of a leadership contest and seemed discredited by scandals affecting two of its leadership candidates.
- It was the neighbouring constituency to Chancellor Gordon Brown's, who was to play a central role in Labour's by-election campaign.

The campaign centred on local issues, including plans to increase toll charges on the Forth Road Bridge and the recent decision of a US computer company to close. Yet the result (see Table 4.1) still came as a huge shock to Labour — and most media commentators.

Candidate	Number of votes	
W. Rennie (Lib Dem)	12391	(36%)
C. Stihler (Lab)	10591	(31%)
D. Chapman (SNP)	7261	(21%)
C. Ruxton (Con)	2702	(8%)
Turnout: 49%		

Table 4.1 **Dunfermline and West Fife by-election result, February 2006**

Assessing Dunfermline and West Fife: a three-party system affirmed?
As indicated already, the by-election did not come at a propitious time for the UK's (then leaderless) third party. Yet, with a swing of 16% in their favour and a 15% increase in their vote share since 2005, this victory ranks with some of the most sensational by-elections ever recorded by Liberal Democrats. Indeed, with the party stalling at national level, the result offered clear proof that Liberal Democrat support — and the UK's alleged three-party system — was more rooted than many believed.

Assessing Dunfermline and West Fife: a dominant party system?
By the same token, there was little to suggest that UK politics is still dominated by New Labour. For Labour's vote share to fall from 46% at the general

election to just 31%, in one of Labour's safest Scottish seats, showed that huge numbers of traditional Labour supporters were deserting the party. With Blair's probable successor playing a major part in its by-election campaign, Labour's decline may not be so easily reversed at the next general election.

Assessing Dunfermline and West Fife: a revived two-party system?

The Conservatives were quick to make light of this result, claiming that the constituency had never been their sort of territory. However, a genuinely resurgent party, destined for government, tends to make some advance almost everywhere. Instead, the Tories came a lamentable fourth and almost lost their deposit on a reduced vote share. Consequently, this result did nothing to alter their reputation as a southern English party no longer able to speak for the UK — a severe hindrance in their bid to look credible again as a party of government.

Assessing Dunfermline and West Fife: a multi-party system?

The multi-party system thesis was not served by this election, with few signs of burgeoning support for either the Scottish National Party or the Scottish Socialist Party. The SNP, whose total vote fell from 2005, was particularly disappointed that the anti-Labour protest vote did not come its way (there were only 500 votes between the SNP and the Liberal Democrats at the general election). So the SNP was not confirmed as a growing force in Scottish working-class constituencies.

The English council elections: great news for the Conservatives?

On 4 May, local elections were held in 176 local authorities. All seats were contested in the 32 London boroughs, a third of seats were contested in 36 other metropolitan boroughs, 20 unitary authorities and 81 non-metropolitan districts, while half the seats were contested in a further seven non-metropolitan districts. National issues — particularly the travails of Blair's government — had considerable effect on the campaign. Yet, in most areas, local activists and local media claimed that it was local issues that were central.

Table 4.2 shows the main parties' overall vote share in the 4 May elections, and the elections' effects on the councils concerned.

Party	Percentage of votes cast (%)	Control of councils contested	
Conservative	39	68	(+11)
Labour	26	30	(−17)
Liberal Democrat	25	13	(+1)
Others	10		
NOC*	—	65	(+5)
Turnout: 37%			

* NOC = 'No overall control', that is, a 'hung' council, where no party has a majority.

Table 4.2 Party vote shares and control of councils contested, 4 May 2006 (2002 figures in brackets)

There was much electoral volatility between 2002 and 2006, resulting in 37 different councils changing control on 4 May 2006. Table 4.3 gives details of councils that changed hands. The overall picture of UK local government after 4 May 2006 (i.e. taking into account those councils and seats not contested on 4 May) is shown in Table 4.4.

Party gains and losses	Councils
Conservative gains from Labour	Bexley, Crawley, Croydon, Ealing, Hammersmith-Fulham
Conservative gains from NOC	Bassetlaw, Chorley, Coventry, Harrow, Hastings, Havering, Hillingdon, Mole Valley, Shrewsbury-Atcham, Winchester
Conservative losses to NOC	Gosport, Harrogate, West Lindsey
Labour gains from NOC	Lambeth
Labour losses to NOC	Barrow-in-Furness, Brent, Bury, Camden, Derby, Hounslow, Lewisham, Merton, Newcastle-under-Lyme, Plymouth, Redditch, Stoke, Warrington
Lib Dem gains from Conservatives	Richmond-upon-Thames
Lib Dem gains from NOC	South Lakeland, St Albans
Lib Dem losses to NOC	Islington, Milton Keynes

Table 4.3 Changes in council control, 2006

Party	Councils controlled	Councillors
Conservative	169 (38%)	8482 (39%)
Labour	73 (17%)	6105 (28%)
Liberal Democrat	34 (8%)	4708 (22%)
Others	17 (4%)	2597 (11%)
NOC	147 (33%)	

Table 4.4 Composition of UK local government after 4 May 2006

Assessing the local elections: a revived two-party system?

For the idea of a two-party system to be plausible, there has to be clear evidence that the main opposition is capable of winning power outright. While acknowledging that they still have a long way to travel, senior Tories claimed that the local elections — the first substantial test of David Cameron's leadership — showed clear signs that their party was on course for government, which brought cheer to the party following the deflating result in Dunfermline.

- The party's vote share (39%) was its best in any set of nationwide elections since 1992. Furthermore, its vote lead over Labour (13%) more than matched the lead it will need at the next general election (10%) if it is to gain a majority of seats.
- Under a two-party system, a swing against the governing party should lead to a corresponding swing towards the main opposition party. There were signs of this in May, with Labour suffering a net loss of 320 seats and the Tories having a net gain of 317.

- The Tories' recovery was not confined to the south, with the party gaining control of Coventry, Bassetlaw and Chorley. They also picked up seats in northern metropolitan areas such as Wigan, Rochdale and Bury, all pointing to a party now winning the national support needed to regain power.
- The Tories became the strongest party in English local government, controlling more councils than Labour and the Liberal Democrats combined.
- The Tories' gains seemed to vindicate Cameron's modernising strategy and helped silence doubters inside his own party. As a result, the party was able to sustain the outward unity so vital to winning power. In a YouGov poll a week later, only 27% of voters saw the Tories as 'divided' (10 years earlier, the figure had been over 70%).

However, Tory celebrations were tempered by two factors:

- The Conservatives made no progress in urban, metropolitan authorities such as Manchester, Liverpool and Newcastle. Given the party's near-collapse in Wales and Scotland, its weakness in English cities could prove fatal at the next general election, as Cameron freely acknowledged.
- The Conservatives' vote share was only slightly higher than in the local elections of 2000 and 2004 (38%, 37%), just a year before the party crashed to defeat at the 2001 and 2005 general elections. The Tories should also recall that the turnout was about 20% lower than in recent general elections — many of the abstainers might return to vote against the Tories at a general election.

Assessing the local elections: a dominant party system?

Afflicted by various scandals and setbacks (John Prescott's affair with a civil servant was first reported during the campaign), Labour knew that it would suffer some losses. Nonetheless, the net loss of 17 councils and 320 seats, plus a national vote share of just 26%, did not suggest a party whose 'dominance' is assured. The aforementioned YouGov poll found that 83% of voters thought Labour was 'divided' — a huge increase since 2005, and the sort of figure usually linked to a doomed party.

There were just two crumbs of comfort for the 'dominant party system' thesis:

- In two urban areas — Manchester and Lambeth — Labour support actually increased, implying that, away from the Westminster treadmill, Labour still has some steady support.
- Labour's vote share was equally poor at the 2004 local elections and even worse at the 1999 European elections, but it still went on to win general elections. With turnout much lower than at a general election, especially in core Labour areas, it is not unreasonable to assume that, in a more critical poll, many abstainers will return to Labour's fold.

Assessing the local elections: three-party system affirmed?

With a net gain of one council, the elections were a 'stand-still' result for the Liberal Democrats: an unsatisfactory outcome for a party that relies heavily on momentum.

However, following the loss of a leader and an embarrassing leadership contest, the elections did come at a difficult time for the UK's third party.

For this reason, Liberal Democrat leaders said that they were generally pleased with the council results, claiming that they embedded a three-party system. The Liberal Democrats highlighted the following:

- They still control over 30 local authorities (e.g. Stockport), as well as having a share of power in most of the 147 'hung' councils.
- They managed to gain control of three councils. Their gain of Richmond-upon-Thames — from a resurgent Tory party — suggests that there will still be more than one serious opposition at the next general election.

Assessing the local elections: a multi-party system?

The kaleidoscopic nature of modern party politics was amply demonstrated in May 2006:

- The British National Party now has 44 councillors and became the main opposition party in Barking and Dagenham (where it won 11 of the 13 seats that it contested). The BNP also won seats in Stoke, Epping Forest, Sandwell, Leeds, Solihull, Redditch, Redbridge and Pendle, strengthening its claim to be a 'nationwide' party.
- The Greens won nine seats, including five in Lewisham.
- Respect won 11 seats in Tower Hamlets, thus cementing its base in the poorer areas of London.
- There are now 2597 councillors from outside the main three parties, while various 'others' control no fewer than 17 councils.

In short, the increasingly complicated character of party competition shows no sign of abating.

The mayoral elections: Labour's southern comfort?

On the same day as the council elections, mayoral elections were held in four boroughs. Conducted under the supplementary vote (SV) electoral system, candidates had to win a majority of first-preference votes to be automatically elected. Otherwise, all but the top two candidates were eliminated, with the second-preference votes of those who supported other candidates reallocated where possible. The results of the mayoral elections held on 4 May are revealed in Table 4.5.

Assessing the mayoral elections: a dominant party system?

Labour was relieved at the mayoral results, especially as its performance in the other local elections was poor. In three of the four contests, Labour's incumbent mayors were re-elected with almost half the first-preference votes, dampening fears that Labour was vulnerable in 'working-class London' (a fear fuelled by the loss of Bethnal Green and Bow to Respect a year earlier).

Assessing the mayoral elections: a revived two-party system?

Conversely, Conservative joy with the council results was tempered by these elections. Cameron stated before the May elections that, to regain credibility, his party would have to re-establish a substantial base in poorer areas. Yet in none of the four boroughs could the Tories secure even a quarter of first-preference votes, and they were pushed into third place in two of them. In the one borough where they qualified for second round (Hackney), they seemed to attract few second-preference votes from Liberal Democrat supporters — the very people that Cameron's 'compassionate Conservatism' is designed to attract.

Borough	Candidate	1st pref. votes	2nd pref. votes	Total
Hackney	J. Pipe (Lab)	20 830	3 403	24 233
	A. Boff (Con)	7 454	1 331	8 785
	M. Penhaligon (Lib Dem)	4 882		
	M. Bone (Green)	4 683		
	H. Peters (Ind)	2 907		
	D. Ryan (Respect)	2 800		
	M. Goldman (Communist)	896		
Turnout: 34%				
Lewisham	S. Bullock (Lab)	22 156	2 974	25 130
	C. Maines (Lib Dem)	12 398	6 491	18 889
	J. Cleverly (Con)	10 790		
	M. Keogh (Green)	7 168		
	J. Hamilton (Ind)	4 823		
	S. Mani (Lewisham People's Alliance)	1 366		
Turnout: 33%				
Newham	R. Wales (Lab)	28 655	5 406	34 061
	A. Jafar (Respect)	12 898		
	S. Choudhury (Con)	8 822		
	A. Craig (Christian People's Alliance)	6 559		
	A. Hussein (Lib Dem)	2 886		
Turnout: 34%				
Watford	D. Thornhill (Lib Dem)	11 963		
	S. O'Brien (Con)	4 838		
	R. Ellis (Lab)	4 062		
	S. Rackett (Green)	2 522		
Turnout: 39%				

Table 4.5 Mayoral elections, 4 May 2006

Assessing the mayoral elections: a three-party system?

Belief in a three-party system would not have been diminished by these results. The Liberal Democrat mayor secured re-election in Watford with an increased share of the vote, while the party's candidate in Lewisham increased his vote share by 5%, overtaking the Tories into second place and winning three times as many second-preference votes as the Labour mayor. The party's vote slipped in Hackney, however, while the result in Newham showed that the Liberal Democrats are not the only home for protest voters, with their candidate being pushed into fifth place with just 5% of the votes.

Assessing the mayoral elections: a multi-party system?

The performance of Respect in Newham — second, with 22% of first-preference votes — indicates that this new party is still progressing in Labour's London heartland. Its candidate would also have been pleased to attract nearly 3000 second-preference votes, suggesting that Respect does not appeal simply to the ultra-left. The Greens also obtained over 10% of first-preference votes in three of the four elections, while the scope for new parties was further revealed in Newham, where the Christian People's Alliance won 11% of first-preference votes (outstripping the Liberal Democrats).

The SV (supplementary vote) system vindicated?

Fans of electoral reform may argue that supplementary vote emerged with credit from these elections. In three of the four elections, it prevented a candidate from winning with only a minority of votes, ensuring that the elected mayors could claim a wider mandate from their constituents. SV's critics, however, might make two points:

- There is no evidence (as electoral reformers argue) that, by making more ballot papers 'count', new electoral systems will increase turnout. The average turnout in these elections was just 36%, no better than that recorded in the council elections, which are held under first-past-the-post.
- Unlike second ballot or alternative vote, this type of majoritarian representation does not guarantee the victor a majority. In Lewisham, the successful candidate finished with 25 130 votes, representing only 42% of those who voted. This is because, under SV, second-preference votes count only if they are cast for the surviving two candidates; in Lewisham, about two-thirds of these votes were not, and were accordingly discarded.

Mayoral elections? Not in Crewe and Nantwich!

Before leaving the issue of mayoral elections, it is worth reporting that, on the same day as the local elections, Crewe and Nantwich Borough Council held a referendum on whether to have an elective mayor of its own. Following the Local Government Act 2000, this was the thirtieth example of a 'trigger ballot' in the UK — one that allows a referendum on elective mayors if 5% of eligible voters petition for one. Such a petition was finalised in November 2005, leading to the less than succinct question in Table 4.6. The result indicated little hunger for either elective mayors or direct democracy.

Are you in favour of the proposal for Crewe and Nantwich Borough Council to be run in a new way, which includes a mayor, elected by the voters of the Borough, to be in charge of its Council services and to lead Crewe and Nantwich Borough Council and the community it serves?	
Yes	**No**
11 808 (39%)	18 768 (61%)
Turnout: 35%	

Table 4.6 The Crewe-Nantwich referendum, 4 May 2006

The Blaenau Gwent by-elections: Labour in meltdown?

Following the death of Peter Law, the Welsh constituency of Blaenau Gwent faced a double by-election on 29 June, Law being not just its MP but also its representative in the Welsh Assembly. Law had originally been Labour's representative in one of the most viscerally Labour seats in Wales (Labour legends such as Bevan and Foot being among his predecessors). Having been de-selected in 2005 by a Labour machine wishing to impose a female candidate, Law then fought and won the seat as an independent, deftly exploiting the area's belief that New Labour — in both its politics and organisation — was a betrayal of south Wales working-class values.

The 2006 by-elections marked a resumption of this New Labour/Old Labour battle, with both seats fought by prominent independents close to Law: his wife, Trish, stood for the Assembly seat, while his former constituency Labour party agent, Dai Davies, stood for Westminster. Small wonder that the election was dubbed a 'family feud'. More remarkable was that Labour lost both elections so badly (Table 4.7).

Election	Candidate	Votes	
Parliamentary	D. Davies (Ind)	12543	(46%)
	O. Smith (Lab)	10059	(37%)
	S. Lewis (Plaid Cymru)	1755	(6.4%)
	A. Kitchener (Lib Dem)	1477	(5.4%)
	M. Williams (Con)	1013	(3.7%)
Welsh Assembly	T. Law (Ind)	13785	(50%)
	J. Hopkins (Lab)	9231	(34%)
	S. Bard (Lib Dem)	2054	(7%)
	J. Price (Plaid Cymru)	1109	(4%)
	J. Burns (Con)	816	(3%)
	J. Matthews (Green)	302	(1%)
Turnout: 52%			

Table 4.7 Blaenau Gwent by-elections, 29 June 2006

Assessing Blaenau Gwent: a dominant party system?

As in Dunfermline and West Fife, Blaenau Gwent suggested that Labour was not so much dominant as disintegrating, failing to regain a parliamentary seat that it held with a 19 000 majority in 2001. Labour's failure to win the Welsh Assembly seat was also startling, given that it won 70% of the votes in the Assembly elections of 2003. Labour had not been complacent in the run-up to the poll, spending over £200 000 on its campaign. While allowing for the 'family feud' aspect, the loss of such safe seats caused much consternation in Labour's ranks, heightening calls for Blair's resignation as Labour leader.

Assessing Blaenau Gwent: a multi-party system?

Conversely, the success of independents will have given much encouragement to smaller parties everywhere. Blaenau Gwent — an area once defined by Labour politics — again showed that even the most tribal of voters are now prepared to cut loose from conventional parties. In both by-elections, almost a majority of voters backed the independent candidate.

Assessing Blaenau Gwent: a revived two-party system?

In respect of the Tories, the message of Dunfermline applied equally in Blaenau Gwent: there are absolutely no signs of Conservative recovery outside England. Again, a party that comes fifth in two elections and wins less than 5% of votes in both scarcely looks poised for power.

The Bromley and Chislehurst by-election: the end of Cameron's honeymoon?

On the same day as the Blaenau Gwent elections, voters in a very different type of constituency (in suburban Kent) also returned a new MP. The Bromley and Chislehurst by-election was caused by the death of Tory MP Eric Forth, a man who had robust Eurosceptic views and who was publicly critical of Cameron's liberal agenda.

As in Blaenau Gwent, there had been friction caused by the main party's choice of candidate. Party Chairman Francis Maude had been keen for local Tories to choose a candidate from Maude's 'A-list', designed to bring in more young, female and black Tories. The Bromley and Chislehurst Tory party resented this and duly chose a 'non-Cameron' candidate, Bob Neill. But this did not end the candidate problem, as Neill was known to have pro-European views at odds with those of local Tory voters. Clearly, this was not an untroubled campaign for the Tories, but the effects were worse than they envisaged (Table 4.8).

Candidate	Number of votes
B. Neill (Con)	11,621 (40%)
B. Abbotts (Lib Dem)	10,988 (38%)
N. Farage (UKIP)	2,347 (8%)
R. Reeves (Lab)	1,925 (6%)
Others (7)	2,171 (8%)
Turnout: 40.5%	

Table 4.8 Bromley and Chislehurst by-election, 29 June 2006

Bromley and Chislehurst assessed: a revived two-party system?

In the words of the *Daily Telegraph*'s Simon Heffer, 'Traditionally, even the dogs vote Tory in Bromley'. So for the Conservative Party, supposedly resurgent under Cameron's leadership, this was a worrying result. Their majority was slashed from 13,342 at the general election to a mere 633, while their share of the vote fell by a fifth. The result lent weight to the view of former Tory Chairman Lord Tebbit, who argued that Cameron's 'Blair-lite' Conservatism would alienate core Tory voters, while failing to convince those who had been voting Labour or Liberal Democrat. In the light of this result, the Tories faced an uncomfortable question: if they struggled to *retain* seats like this one, at a time when neither Labour nor Liberal Democrats were prospering, how could they hope to *gain* seats at the next general election?

Those who argue for a revived two-party system might also consider that, in the two constituencies holding by-elections on 29 June, just 44% of voters backed either of the two main parties.

Bromley and Chislehurst assessed: a three-party system?

As in Dunfermline, this result proved that the Liberal Democrats remain a serious force, even after the debacle of their leadership change. On a reduced turnout, the Liberal Democrats' total vote still rose, while their vote share doubled since the general election. That they leapfrogged Labour, which had been second at the general election, confirmed that in large parts of the south they had eclipsed Labour as the main alternative to the Tories.

Bromley and Chislehurst assessed: a dominant party system?

The constituency had always been a lost cause for Labour, but it was still a depressing result for a party that came to power by impressing swathes of southern, middle-class voters. With its vote share plummeting by two-thirds, Labour fell from second to fourth and came within 1% of losing its deposit. New Labour's claim to dominance rests upon 'inclusive' support and 'catch-all' appeal. However, neither was evident at this by-election.

Bromley and Chislehurst assessed: a multi-party system?

That Labour was beaten by UKIP showed that, in many seats, the two main parties are not troubled just by the Liberal Democrats: they have to fight a wider campaign to dismiss a number of fringe parties. With their Europhile candidate, Tories in Bromley had to address the additional threat of UKIP, whose candidate was one of its national leaders. On the other hand, UKIP should have done better given the nature of the constituency, the legacy of its former MP and the politics of the Tory candidate. It may have come third, but it still won only 8% of the votes.

Conclusion: towards a 'post-British' party system?

Four clear messages emerge from the various elections of 2006:

(1) Labour is phenomenally unpopular. Consequently, we should be wary of endorsing the 'dominant party system' idea, even though Labour did endure comparable unpopularity before both 2001 and 2005.

(2) Tory progress is limited. We should also be cautious about accepting claims that the Tories are now heading inexorably to power, thus rescuing the notion of a two-party system. Despite a decent performance in the council elections, their performance in all the others was at best mediocre and, in some cases, dismal. If Labour falls from office, a hung parliament could be the most likely outcome, especially as the Liberal Democrats seem to have weathered their internal difficulties.

(3) Voter apathy remains a huge problem. Only in the Blaenau Gwent elections did a majority of those eligible vote, and even here over 40% abstained. In assessing the UK's party system, we need to remember that the bulk of voters now seem indifferent to all the UK's parties. Indeed, can we legitimately talk about a democratic 'party system' when most voters seem disconnected from party politics?

(4) Party competition is now irregular and pattern-less. Some good examples of this message came in the council elections. Labour, despite performing badly nationwide, did well in Manchester; the Tories, despite making big gains in London, still managed to lose control of Richmond-upon-Thames; the Liberal Democrats, despite winning that particular London borough, managed to lose another in Islington.

According to Professor Anthony King, the 2006 elections simply confirm a 'variable party system', where the key party battle differs from one area to the next. In Dunfermline and West Fife, there was a battle between Labour, the Liberal Democrats and the SNP; in Bromley, one between the Tories, the Liberal Democrats and UKIP; in Newham, one between Labour and Respect, and so on.

What this suggests, however, is that the UK's two-party system has not been replaced by anything so clear cut as a three-party system or a multi-party system. Indeed, we may have no *British* party system at all, just a series of endless fluctuations driven by peculiar local circumstances. In view of the 2006 elections, the case for a *localised* or *post-British* party system seems quite compelling.

Summary

- Labour haemorrhaged support.
- Tory progress was limited.
- The Liberal Democrats lost momentum but remain credible.
- Small parties and independents continued to impress.
- Low turnout remained a concern.
- The nature of the UK's party system is unresolved, but...
- ...theories of a 'localised' party system are persuasive.

Funding political parties: an intractable problem?

About this chapter

The funding of political parties resurfaced as a serious political issue in 2006, prompted mainly by the 'cash for peerages' scandal engulfing the Labour Party. Indeed, it developed into one of the most sensational political topics of modern times — the 'British Watergate' in one journalist's words — threatening both the arrest of a sitting prime minister and the toppling of a government. Unsurprisingly, the year saw a spate of inquiries into party funding and a range of proposed reforms. In this chapter, we will see why party finance is a problem and inspect some of the 'solutions' put forward. We will answer questions such as:

- Why are parties thought to have insufficient revenue?

- What are the current sources of party revenue and why do they seem 'sleazy'?

- Should there be more state assistance in the funding of political parties?

- Should there be a limit on how much individuals can donate to parties?

Why is the funding of political parties a problem?

There seem to be two broad factors that make party funding a problem, both of which were brought into focus during 2006:
- Parties are thought to have insufficient revenue.
- Current sources of party revenue seem unfair and 'sleazy'.

Both these factors will be examined in some detail in this chapter.

Why are parties thought to have insufficient revenue?

A straightforward examination of the main parties' accounts suggests serious under-funding:
- *The Conservative Party*. In July 2006, it was revealed that the Conservative Party had run up debts of almost £15 million in the aftermath of the 2005 general election. According to party treasurer Lord Marland, this figure was 'not unexpected', given that the party's costs rose from £15 million in a typical, non-election year to £39 million as a result of the 2005 general election campaign and its year-long build-up (see Table 5.1).
- *The Labour Party*. With a whiff of understatement, Labour Chairman Hazel Blears admitted her party's accounts were 'in a fairly challenging position'. In fact, Labour in 2006 appeared to have an unprecedented debt totalling almost £28 million (involving £13 million owed to banks from conventional loans,

plus a further £13 million in loans from 12 wealthy businessmen — see p. 50). As with the Tories, spending on the general election was held responsible for this precarious position. One Labour official described the party as 'woefully insolvent', while a leading insolvency expert observed that 'if Labour were a company, you would have to question its continued ability to trade' (*Daily Telegraph*, 21 August 2006). By the summer of 2006, Labour was forced to sell its Old Queen Street headquarters and there were rumours that the party could not pay the salaries of its 230 full-time officials.

- *The Liberal Democrat Party*. The third party's financial crisis was not so acute, mainly because it spent only a quarter of what Labour and the Tories spent on the 2005 general election. Nonetheless, its debts still totalled £207 000, prompting Lord Razzall (its chief fundraiser) to admit that the party was 'running on a shoestring' (*Daily Telegraph*, 19 July 2006).

Party	Income	Expenditure
Labour	£35 312 000	£49 809 000
Conservative	£24 241 000	£39 238 000
Liberal Democrats	£5 121 121	£4 914 418
UKIP	£1 744 659	£1 702 549
Respect	£497 565	£589 789
Green	£473 224	£506 543

Table 5.1 Budgets of main political parties, 2005/06

But why are there such huge debts? There are six explanations for the parties' deficits:

(1) Parties are fighting more elections than ever. European elections, devolution elections and (in some urban areas) mayoral elections can now be added to the cost of parliamentary and council campaigns. UK parties, like their US counterparts, seem in a state of 'permanent campaign'.

(2) Dealignment. In recent decades, fewer and fewer voters have identified with any of the major parties. This has three financial consequences for party organisers:

- *More effort has to be made to target the electorate.* Gone are the days when parties could rely on huge armies of support — more must be spent on party campaigns to attract voters. The parties are struggling to meet this requirement. According to Lord Marland, by 2006, the Tories still lacked 'adequate resources to reach the voters we need', while Lord Razzall made the interesting point (in May) that 'no party can now rely on a single nationwide campaign...the electorate is more volatile and regionalised, so we now need to fund, somehow, a variety of regional campaigns as well as a national one'.
- *Parties have fewer members.* By 2006, Labour and the Conservatives had fewer than half a million members between them (Labour's membership fell by 50% between 1997 and 2006). Fewer members, of course, means fewer

subscriptions: by 2006, Labour raised just 8% of its income from member subscriptions, the Conservatives 10% and the Liberal Democrats 30%. Fewer members also means less income from the 'social' side of party activities (the income from the bars of Conservative clubs fell by 30% between 2001 and 2006) and a narrower range of fundraising activity.

- *More needs to be spent on policy research.* With fewer voters ready to lend instinctive support, parties may have to devote more resources to developing attractive policies. As Labour's chief fundraiser, Lord Levy, told the House of Commons Constitutional Affairs Select Committee in June 2006, 'We have to spend more on finding out what voters want and working out how to give it to them'.

(3) The end of the Cold War and the end of the left/right ideological battle. Though welcomed by Conservatives, this has gravely hindered their fundraising. With an almost universal acceptance of capitalism, and with Labour having ditched its commitment to public ownership, business no longer sees such a pressing need for Conservative governments. As a result, the Conservatives have suffered what Lord Marland termed (in March 2006) 'a haemorrhage of corporate support for the party'. Company donations, which formed about 60% of Conservative central income in 1981, were said to represent just 30% by 2006.

(4) Decline of heavy industry. Whereas in 1970 33% of the workforce was in manufacturing, today the figure is just 14%. This has brought about a steep decline in trade union membership (from 13 million in 1979 to about 9 million today), which has made it harder for trade unions to give generously to the Labour Party.

(5) The Political Parties, Elections and Referendums Act 2000. This Act obliges parties to publish the names of those donating over £5000 to a political party. But as Professor Vernon Bogdanor noted in his 2006 Gresham Lecture, 'Would-be donors have been deterred by public association with a party...while those in line for an honour might be concerned lest it seem tarnished'. Events of 2006 concerning loans to the Labour Party (see the next section) are unlikely to make wealthy individuals keener to sponsor political parties.

(6) Wasteful spending. According to Simon Jenkins of *The Times*, 'party officials have watched too many episodes of *The West Wing*' (the popular US television drama about White House politics) and have been lured into financing opulent offices, huge secretariats and lavish campaigns, exemplified by Labour's engorged party payroll (£12.8 million by 2006), the cost of its 2005 campaign headquarters (£3 million, compared with its normal buildings costs of £1.6 million) and its spending spree during the year of the 2005 general election (£14.5 million, compared with £2.6 million in 2004).

The Tories have been no less culpable in this respect. To symbolise a break with their Thatcherite past, they recently moved from their Smith Square headquarters into state-of-the-art offices in London's Victoria Street. However, they failed either to sell or to rent out Smith Square before moving, resulting in losses of £5.5 million by the end of 2006.

Why do current sources of party revenue seem unfair and sleazy?

There seem to be three explanations: inequality of revenue, the nature of state funding and the nature of non-state funding.

Inequality of revenue

Individual donations lead to huge disparities of income between the main parties. This has proved especially harsh on the Liberal Democrats who, during the 2005 campaign, were able to spend only approximately a quarter of the amount spent by their two main rivals. Yet, even between the 'big two', there are significant disparities in both income and spending. Although Labour's revenue surpassed the Tories' in the run-up to the 2005 general election, the Conservative Party usually benefits far more from donations and loans (see Tables 5.3 and 5.4). During the first 3 months of 2006, the Conservatives received over £8 million worth

Donor	Amount
Roger Gabb	£500 000
G. Pinto	£100 000
Lord Steinberg	£530 000
Michael Stone	£100 000
Harris Ventures Ltd	£50 000
Moorlake Properties	£50 000
Lord Ashcroft	£50 000
A. R. Said	£50 000

Note: Robert Edmiston's 2005 loan of £2 million was later converted into a donation.

Table 5.2 Principal Tory donors, January–March 2006

of donations (see Table 5.2 for the principal donors), compared with Labour's £2.8 million and the Liberal Democrats' £683 744. Labour may have about a dozen millionaire backers, but the Tories are said to have 30–50 backers prepared to make six-figure donations.

This inequality was tempered by the Political Parties, Elections and Referendums Act 2000, which compelled parties to disclose donations of over £5000 while limiting national campaign spending to approximately £19 million per party. Yet the Tories overcame this problem, and maintained their financial superiority, by:

- relying more on loans, which are not subject to the Act (the Tories' loans for 2005 were about £6 million greater than Labour's)
- switching their campaign spending from national to local level. In each constituency, candidates can spend up to a certain figure, depending on the number of constituents (the figure is usually between £10 000 and £13 000). In 2005, the Tories spent the maximum amount allowed in 80% of constituencies, whereas Labour did so in 61% and the Liberal Democrats in 44%. In short, the Tories still managed to spend substantially more on the 2005 campaign than their main rivals.
- spreading substantial expenditure over the course of a whole parliament, rather than simply during a general election campaign. Helped by regular, hefty donations from Lord Ashcroft, the Conservatives are thought to have

spent (during the last parliament) twice the amount spent by Labour in key marginal seats.

This financial advantage must be kept in perspective, of course: the Tories have still lost the last three general elections and have failed in each to gain even a third of the votes cast.

The nature of state funding

The second reason for criticising current funding methods relates to the sources of state aid — notably 'Short Money' and 'Cranborne Money' — distributed to opposition parties at Westminster to help with their parliamentary business. Because the money is calculated on the basis of a party's seats rather than its votes, and because our electoral system is not proportional, this system seems to penalise the Liberal Democrats. In 2005/06, the Conservatives received over £4 million in Short Money and £425 000 in Cranborne Money, while the Liberal Democrats got approximately £1.5 million and £210 000. In other words, although the Tories did not get twice as much support as the Liberal Democrats at the last general election, they ended up with nearly three times as much state assistance. So, in its present form, state aid may just be propping up a moribund two-party system.

The nature of non-state funding

The most obvious factor behind the unattractive nature of party funding — and spectacularly evident in 2006 — concerns the parties' dependency on 'plutocratic' revenue: that is, income derived from a small group of wealthy individuals. In 2006, it emerged that about £14 million of the £17 million Labour spent on its 2005 general election campaign came from the loans of 12 businessmen, while approximately 60% of Conservative revenue came from about 20 individual loans (see Tables 5.3 and 5.4).

Lender	Position	Amount
Sir David Garrard	Founder of Minerva property group	£2.3m
Lord Sainsbury	Member of the Sainsbury supermarket dynasty	£2m
Richard Caring	Clothing magnate	£2m
Dr Chai Patel	Executive of Priory health group	£1.5m
Rod Aldridge	Chairman of Capita	£1m
Nigel Morris	Founder of Capital One	£1m
Andrew Rosenfeld	Executive of Minerva property group	£1m
Barry Townsley	Stockbroker	£1m
Sir Christopher Evans	Founder of Merlin Biosciences	£1m
Gordon Crawford	Founder of London Bridge Software Holdings	£500 000
Derek Tullett	Founder of Tullett Liberty stockbrokers	£400 000
Sir Gulam Noon	Founder of the food company Noon Products	£250 000

Table 5.3 Substantial loans to Labour, 2005

Donor	Position	Amount
Lord Ashcroft	Former Party Chair	£3.5m
Michael Hintze	Hedge fund consultant	£2.5m
Robert Edmiston	Car dealer	£2m
Arbuthnot Latham	City banker	£2m
Johan Eliasch	Sportswear magnate	£1m

Table 5.4 Hefty loans to the Conservative Party, 2005

The main parties' reliance on rich benefactors stems from four developments:
- increased election expenditure
- declining membership
- declining corporate support (notably in respect of the Conservatives)
- Labour's wish to end its reliance on trade unions and thus broaden its electoral support

This new reliance on rich individuals causes six interrelated problems, all of which were highlighted — often in sensational fashion — during 2006:

(1) It makes party funding unpredictable. Many of the parties' individual donors have proved 'fair-weather friends'. (A notable omission from Table 5.3 is Formula 1 chief, Bernie Ecclestone, who gave Labour £1 million in the late 1990s but has offered nothing since.) As a result, the parties' incomes are volatile and capricious, causing difficulties in making any long-term financial plans. By 2006, Labour was again receiving 75% of its income from trade unions — the very situation that Blairites had tried to avoid by cultivating rich benefactors.

(2) It is secretive and dubious. It is estimated that, before the last general election, the two main parties secured up to £37 million of revenue secretly (*Daily Telegraph*, 16 July 2006). Although the 2000 Act brought more openness to individual *donations*, the two main parties have circumvented this by taking out furtive *loans*. In March 2006, Labour Party Treasurer Jack Dromey revealed that he had known nothing of the loans detailed in Table 5.3 and complained that 'elected officers of the Labour Party are being kept in the dark about our fundraising'. It transpired that Dromey had been side-tracked by Lord Levy, who had (allegedly) been mandated by Blair to solicit huge loans for Labour — loans that, many suspect, would eventually become *de facto* donations. According to the Electoral Commission (set up by the 2000 Act to police party finance), these loans may not have been illegal, but were 'improper' and 'at odds with the legislation'. As Table 5.4 shows, the Conservatives were no less culpable in this respect, receiving up to £20 million in loans prior to the last general election. The details of these loans were disclosed only after the party faced an exhaustive inquiry by the Electoral Commission, and it later admitted that some of them were from residents overseas — another example of the law's 'spirit' being broken by parties (foreign donations being illegal under the 2000 Act). The Liberal Democrats were also brought into disrepute by this type of revenue: property tycoon Michael Brown, who gave them £2.4 million for the last general election, was later jailed for fraud, forgery and false accounting.

(3) It gives the impression that parties can be 'bought'. Voters may surmise that government policy is shaped by the interests of those sponsoring the party in power, rather than by the common good. It was revealed in March 2006, for example, that Capita — the firm of Labour's lender Rod Aldridge (see Table 5.3) — has benefited from the government's multimillion-pound public sector contracts, including the management of London's congestion charge. The Aldridge case has strong echoes of the Ecclestone donation 8 years earlier, when motor racing was later exempted from the government's ban on tobacco sponsorship in sport, and the government's award of a £32 million contract to Powderject (to develop a smallpox vaccine) shortly after its director donated £50 000 to Labour in 2002.

(4) It debases the honours system. Thanks to the nature of modern party finance, in 2006 it seemed that a place in the Lords owed little to disinterested public service. In fact, during 2006, British politics was almost defined by talk of 'cash for peerages' and 'loans for lordships', leading to a clique of 'Tony's cronies' in the upper chamber. Amid suspicions that their nominations stemmed from them lending money to the Labour Party, the peerage nominations of Sir David Garrard and Dr Chai Patel were blocked by the Lords Appointments Commission, while that of Barry Townsley was withdrawn. This leads to the fifth problem…

(5) It reinforces 'sleaze'. Claims that party finance has diminished the integrity of British politics have been especially prevalent under New Labour and certainly predate 2006 (see the cases of Ecclestone, Lakshmi Mittal and the Hinduja brothers). These claims were dramatically reinforced in 2006 by a Scotland Yard inquiry into claims that senior government figures had contravened both the Honours (Prevention of Abuses) Act 1925 and the Political Parties, Elections and Referendums Act 2000 by promising peerages in return for loans to the Labour Party. Following the arrest of Blair's chief fundraiser Lord Levy and the growing possibility that Blair himself would be questioned by police, the press was not slow to see its monumental significance (see Box 5.1). The course of this phenomenal episode is charted in Table 5.5. The 'cash for peerages' debacle reinforced the final, and perhaps most serious, problem with the parties' reliance on wealthy individuals.

(6) It further erodes public confidence in our representative democracy. Although New Labour came to power promising to 'clean up' British politics, and thereby restore voters' faith in the British political system, by 2006 it was clear that it had simply made matters worse. As Table 5.6 reveals, in the wake of Levy's arrest, the number of voters who thought that the government was corrupt was even greater than in 1997, when Tory 'sleaze' (e.g. 'cash for questions') played a big part in the Major administration's downfall.

Box 5.1 **The aftermath of Lord Levy's arrest**

'The sewage is beginning to lap around Tony Blair's ankles. He is poised to become the first sitting prime minister to be questioned by police in connection with a criminal inquiry. Think about how humiliating this is. We are not Italians, and the idea that the Queen's first minister might have been involved in selling places in our legislature is demeaning — and acutely embarrassing — to the entire nation.'

Source: *Sunday Telegraph*, 16 July 2006.

Date	Event
18 January	Des Smith (adviser to government on city academies) caught by undercover reporter suggesting that honours would be given in return for donations
8 March	Chai Patel protests that his peerage nomination has been blocked by Lords Appointments Commission; Barry Townsley (another Labour lender) withdraws his nomination
16 March	Labour's elected treasurer, Jack Dromey, states that he knew nothing of loans to Labour negotiated by Blair ally Lord Levy
17 March	Labour confirms it received £14 million in loans before the general election; Blair admits that he did not inform Lords Appointments Commission
21 March	Scotland Yard launches investigation into loans possibly breaching law on honours
24 March	It emerges that ex-Labour General Secretary Matt Carter wrote to lenders stating that their loans would not have to be declared by the party
27 March	Police ask Commons Public Administration Committee to delay its own inquiry into 'cash for peerages' as it would now be *sub judice*
13 April	Des Smith arrested and bailed
16 May	Lords Appointments Commission says it has been 'kept in dark' over loans to Labour
10 July	It emerges that Gulan Noon was advised by Lord Levy to omit his £250 000 loans to Labour from his application for a peerage
12 July	Lord Levy arrested and questioned by police
20 September	Sir Christopher Evans (founder of Merlin Biosciences and lender of £1 million to Labour in 2005) arrested by police

Table 5.5 Loans, lordships and Labour — chronology of a scandal

1. % agreeing that 'the Government gives the impression of being sleazy and disreputable'

January 1997: 63%   April 2006: 62%   July 2006: 69%

2. Do you suspect that Labour raised money by offering 'cash for peerages'?

Yes: 65%   No: 9%   Don't know: 25%

3. If Labour did raise money in this way, do you suspect that Tony Blair knew?

Yes: 65%   No: 13%   Don't know: 22%

4. Has the Blair government reformed party funding so as to end sleaze?

Yes: 6%   No: 78%   Don't know: 16%

5. Do you think it wrong that those who give loans to parties should not have to declare them?

Yes: 87%   No: 3%   Don't know: 10%

6. Should the legal limits on the parties' campaign spending be further reduced?

Yes: 77%   No: 12%   Don't know: 11%

7. Would further state aid to parties help clean up politics — and would you support public money being spent in this way?

| I think it would help and I support such a move: 25% | I think it would help, but I would not support such a move: 22% | I do not think it would help: 37% | Don't know: 17% |

Source: YouGov, 15 July 2006.

Table 5.6 Sleaze and party funding: the voters' views, 2006

Should the funding of political parties be reformed?

The reform of party finance revolves around three central questions:
- Should there be more state assistance?
- Should there be a cap on donations?
- Should campaign spending limits be altered?

Should there be more state assistance?

Short and Cranborne Monies are not the only ways in which the state already funds UK parties. Indeed, the Electoral Commission told the 2006 POWER inquiry that, in an average year, £25 million of public funds is given to parties, and £111 million in the year of a general election. How are such monies channelled?
- The main parties do not have to pay for their party political broadcasts. At the 2005 general election, this perk was thought to represent £68 million of free advertising for the three main British parties.
- Election candidates are entitled to freepost when contacting electors in their constituencies. In 2005, this scheme was thought to have cost the state about £20 million.

- Since the Political Parties, Elections and Referendums Act 2000, Policy Development Grants are shared among the main parties to assist with their policy research. In 2006, the 'big three' each received approximately £458 000 in PDGs.

The question, therefore, is whether state funding of parties should increase to the more generous levels found in most EU countries.

By 2006, there was growing consensus that state aid should be extended, with even the Conservative Party (traditionally hostile) making supportive noises. The reason for this seems to be a general acceptance that, in Vernon Bogdanor's words, 'a healthy democracy requires healthy political parties', and that healthy parties are possible only if they are:
- less financially challenged
- less reliant upon donations and therefore…
- …more transparent in their financial dealings

During 2006, a number of schemes were put forward by those supporting more state aid, all of them reflecting the anxieties cited above:
- *The POWER inquiry.* Under the chairmanship of Helena Kennedy QC, POWER suggested that up to £90 million of extra public money be made available, and that it should be distributed according to 'explicit public support'. On ballot papers, each voter would be able to tick a box, mandating £3 of public money to a party of his/her choice. That money would fund local party and candidate activity in the voter's constituency. (For more on the POWER inquiry, see Chapter 6.)
- *The Electoral Commission and New Politics Network* (see Box 5.2). Both favoured an extension of freepost funding — providing the literature was produced and distributed by local parties.
- *Vernon Bogdanor's Gresham Lecture.* Bogdanor argued for a Canadian-style system of state aid, linking state funding to membership recruitment. For every £20 a party raised in subscriptions, it would receive a matching £20 from the state. Bogdanor claimed that this would stop parties being complacent about dwindling memberships and provide impetus to local party activity.

Box 5.2 **What is the New Politics Network?**

NPN is a think-tank that, since 2003, has specialised in party funding. Its aim is to link reform to the promotion of local political activity. Its reports include *Strong Parties, Clean Politics* (2003), *Broadening Participation* (2003) and *Life Support for Political Parties* (2004), all accessible via **www.new-politics.net**.

Despite the volume of proposals, there are still serious objections to parties receiving more money from public funds, as Box 5.3 reveals.

More state funding: the case against

- *It rewards profligacy and mismanagement.* As explained earlier, the parties' problems stem to a large extent from their own heavy spending — and, as will be argued at the end of this chapter, such spending may be unnecessary. It seems perverse to argue that the taxpayer should be held responsible for the parties' indulgence.

- *It is a misuse of public money.* When public services seem under-funded, it may be improper to finance more party staffers instead of, say, more teachers and doctors. For this reason…

- *…it could make parties even more unpopular with voters.* As Table 5.6 shows, only a quarter of voters clearly support more state aid, suspecting perhaps that politicians are again 'feathering their own nests'.

- *It may insulate parties from their own unpopularity.* Ironically, if they are made more unpopular by more state aid, the parties — buttressed by hefty subsidies from the taxpayer — may feel less impelled to do something about it.

- *It may fuel the growth of an 'apparatchik' class.* If parties are helped to finance their ever-growing armies of officials, the state will be helping to expand a class of career politicians who have never worked in the 'real world'. This may then lead to more policies that do not chime with voters and thus make parties even more unpopular.

- *It may restrict the choice offered to voters (particularly by the Conservatives).* If all the main parties become the recipients of generous state funding, they may be less inclined to question increased tax and public spending. The neo-liberal, Thatcherite perspective is an important one in UK politics that should be aired to voters. But will Conservatives air it if they, too, are 'clients' of the state? In short, more state aid could strengthen voters' complaints that our main parties are 'all the same'.

- *It has not made party politics healthier elsewhere.* The crisis of party popularity is not a British phenomenon; it also exists in EU countries where state aid is much greater. Indeed, there is a case for saying that, in certain EU countries, 'sleaze' and corruption are even greater issues on account of state subsidies to parties. In France, over 1000 party officials have been convicted for offences under party funding rules, while similar scandals have afflicted Germany, Belgium and Italy. The opportunities for extra state funding, it seems, merely generate different examples of party officials cutting corners and bringing politics into disrepute.

Should there be a cap on donations?

The 'cash for peerages' scandal made this one of the most pressing questions about party funding in 2006. Opinion polls suggested a wish for change: an ICM poll in May found that 74% agreed that there should be a limit on how much individuals can donate to parties. The Electoral Commission also found 70% thinking that, under the status quo, 'wealthy individuals can buy influence over parties'. The following proposals emerged in 2006:

- *The POWER inquiry.* Donations from individuals should be capped at £10 000; organisational donations at £100 per member.
- *New Politics Network.* NPN supported the broad principle of a cap, between £5 000 and £10 000, but was not opposed to larger donations from institutions such as trade unions. Its proviso was that these institutional donations should simply be the sum of voluntary individual donations within the institution concerned, with the institution acting as the 'broker' and facilitator. NPN thought that institutional donations could encourage greater public interest in party politics — as long as there was no element of coercion.
- *The Conservative and Labour parties.* Perhaps stung by his party's involvement in the loans debacle, David Cameron advocated a limit of £50 000 (as well as a ban on all future loans, other than those conducted on strict commercial terms from recognised financial institutions). Labour's National Executive Committee rejected this idea, claiming that it was a 'ruse' to benefit the Tories at Labour's expense: as mentioned earlier, Labour has 12 'mega-donations', which would obviously be precluded by Cameron's scheme, whereas the Tories have a huge number of more modest donations, which would be within this limit. Labour also defended union funding on the grounds that it sprang from 'ideological values, shared by most union members', and that it was legitimised by the Tories' own legislation: the Trade Union Act 1984 requires union donations to be endorsed regularly in a ballot of union members.

Should campaign spending limits be altered?

Although there had been no limits to campaign spending until 2000, by 2006 there was general agreement that some limits were needed to prevent an 'arms race' of escalated spending in election years. For the POWER inquiry, Vernon Bogdanor and the Conservative Party, the existing limits were about right. Others, however, wanted change so as to get 'fairer' electoral competition and greater stress on local campaigning:

- The Labour Party wished to neutralise the Tories' 'mid-term' advantages by setting limits on spending between, as well as during, elections. It did not offer any figures.
- The Electoral Commission suggested a reduction in the national spending limit to £15 million and a proportionate increase in the amount allowed for constituency candidates.
- New Politics Network echoed the above by proposing that national campaign spending be limited to £10 million, but with a 20% increase in the limit for constituency spending.

The Phillips Review

The most important and wide-ranging survey into party finance came with the launch of a government-funded inquiry in March 2006: the Review of the Funding of Political Parties. Chaired by Sir Hayden Phillips, it was the prime minister's own response to the furore generated by 'cash for peerages'. Taking evidence from the political parties, the Electoral Commission, assorted academics and the House of Commons Constitutional Affairs Select Committee, the Phillips inquiry was the most important state assessment of party finance since the Houghton Report 30 years earlier. Indeed, its opening assertion that 'democratic politics depends on credible political parties' echoed Houghton's claim that 'if the parties fail, then democracy fails'.

The Phillips report was particularly keen to address four questions, which were highlighted in its interim report in September:
- How can party funding be made more transparent?
- Should state funding be extended?
- Should campaign funding be limited?
- Should the laws on donations be overhauled?

Phillips's final report was expected in early 2007.

Conclusion: an alternative remedy?

An idea that none of the reform proposals addressed is this: *party politics in the UK needs scaling down*. In other words, the parties' organisations should be streamlined, localised and as a result be made much less expensive.

It is worth asking *why* the parties need to spend the alarming amount that they have spent in recent years. Much has been made of the growing cost of campaigns. But we should note that, as the parties' campaign expenditure has risen so dramatically in recent years, turnout has fallen. As Chapter 4 reveals, one of the most staggering electoral stories of recent years has been the success of independents and other low-budget candidates in places such as Blaenau Gwent. We cannot discount the possibility that the slicker and costlier a campaign, the more distrust it provokes, and the more 'shoestring' and off-beat a campaign, the more voters may empathise with it.

With a view to cutting their spending, the parties might also ask *why* their propaganda has to come from expensive PR agencies, instead of internal talent — especially given our increasingly 'karaoke culture', where earthiness is exalted via 'reality TV', for example — and *why* party political broadcasts have to involve hi-tech films instead of the parties' own spokespeople summarising policies from behind a desk (if they cannot do this deftly, they are probably poor politicians).

Above all, the parties should ask *why* their campaigns are still characterised by glossy centralised operations — complete with party leaders whizzing around in helicopters — instead of more earthy, localised arrangements, where parties put their message in a local context. Once again, the parties may have much to learn from the myriad of grass-roots pressure groups that have emerged in recent years.

Summary

- The current financing of UK parties is a cause for concern.

- This concern was reinforced by the 'cash for peerages' scandal.

- There is a growing demand for more state aid to parties, but...

- ...more state aid might only increase voter disenchantment.

The POWER inquiry: democracy in danger?

About this chapter

The report of POWER, an independent inquiry into the state of UK democracy, was published in February 2006. It represented one of the most wide-ranging surveys of UK democracy in the twenty-first century and recorded a series of disturbing observations. However, though its diagnosis was gloomy, its prognosis was lively, offering a range of radical ideas to revive the flagging representative system. This chapter will answer the following questions:

- What was the POWER inquiry?
- What were POWER's criticisms?
- What were POWER's proposals?

What was the POWER inquiry?

The POWER inquiry was set up in 2004 and funded by the Joseph Rowntree Charitable Trust. It was commissioned to investigate the relationship between voters and existing representative democracy. Central to the inquiry was a belief that the relationship was in crisis and that urgent remedial action was needed to restore it.

The inquiry involved ten commissioners, supported by a small secretariat and research team, and chaired by Helena Kennedy QC. Its work comprised:
- seven meetings across the country
- 143 interviews with assorted experts and affected individuals
- 400 'democracy dinners', allowing interested parties to air views more informally
- a telephone survey of 1000 adults who abstained at the 2005 general election
- a comprehensive survey of relevant literature
- an 'open budget' meeting in the London borough of Harrow

POWER produced what is arguably the most concise survey of UK democracy in the new millennium. Its findings suggest that the existing system is ill at ease with the society it serves.

The POWER report can be divided into two: its criticisms and its proposals. This chapter will inspect both.

What were POWER's criticisms?

The report argued that the UK's representative democracy — centred on political parties, parliamentary elections and parliamentary government — was dangerously out of tune with the character of the British people. British society, it was claimed, had changed dramatically in the last 25 years, yet the formal characteristics of UK democracy had not evolved with it, creating a dangerous dissonance between citizens and state.

POWER highlighted four key problems with representative democracy in the UK today:
- diminishing turnout in elections
- public hostility to political parties
- a sense, among voters, that the political system is unaccountable
- a failure, on the part of the state, to harness new democratic forces in society

POWER evaluated each of these four problems.

Why is electoral turnout diminishing?

POWER had little difficulty in showing that electoral turnout was a problem. At the 2005 general election, only 61% voted — an improvement of just 2% since the 2001 election, which recorded the lowest general election turnout since 1918.

A neat illustration of the problem is that whereas 9.5 million voters backed the most popular party, over 17 million did not vote at all. In other words, the government was endorsed by just 22% of eligible voters. Turnout in local, European and regional elections (e.g. those for the Scottish Parliament and Welsh Assembly) was even worse.

POWER dismissed the idea that low turnout was due to 'the politics of contentment', a view offered by the late Robin Cook shortly after the 2005 election. As POWER pointed out, the logic of this argument is that turnout in deprived urban areas should be higher (whereas it was generally lower), with unskilled working-class voters being among the most enthusiastic (whereas they were among the most reluctant — just 54% of social group D/E voted). Among ethnic minority voters — again, a group not normally linked to a satisfied view of the status quo — turnout was just 47%. In short, there was no cause to be complacent about low electoral turnout.

Why do large numbers of voters abstain? POWER cited four key reasons, based upon interviews with about 1000 abstainers:
- *There is a perception that, in their particular constituency, their vote is wasted — the result being a foregone conclusion.* Forty-nine per cent of the abstainers stated that they 'may well have voted' if their favoured candidate or party had some chance of winning.

- *There is a perception that, whatever the result, governments will pursue their own agenda.* In the words of one non-voter: 'People don't bother voting because in the end politicians will ignore them...people have no real say in what the government does.'
- *There is a perception that the 'broad agenda' choice on offer does not reflect voters' diversity of views.* For example, a voter might agree with Labour on one issue (higher public spending over tax cuts being one example), but support the Conservatives on another (such as immigration). In the words of another abstainer: 'The parties are too broadbrush — I agree with some of their ideas but not others.'
- *There is a sceptical view of the main political parties.* As POWER remarked, 'Few aspects of the political system received more hostile comment than the main political parties.' As such, it devoted a significant section of its report to this particular problem.

Why are voters hostile to the main political parties?

POWER looked at both the symptoms and causes of public disengagement from the main political parties. In terms of symptoms, it pointed to three obvious examples:

- *Declining electoral support.* At the 2005 general election, not one party managed even 40% of the votes cast, with the winning party scraping only 35%. This was no aberration: at the previous year's European elections, no party attained even 30% of the votes. Labour may now claim to be the 'natural party of government', but it should remember that in 2005, fewer people voted for it than in 1987, when Labour lost by a landslide. And while the Conservatives enjoyed a very modest recovery in 2005, their own total vote was still less than in 1997 when they suffered what was then their worst defeat since 1832.
- *Declining voter identification.* Those who still vote for the main parties do so with little relish. In 1964, 44% of voters 'strongly identified' with a political party; by 2005, only 15% did — and remember that this does not include the 39% who did not vote at all.
- *Declining party membership.* Having had almost 5 million members between them in the 1950s, the two main parties had less than half a million by 2005, Labour having lost approximately a quarter of its members since 1997. As POWER noted, overall party membership is now just a quarter of its 1964 levels, involving just 2% of voters. One of the interesting points to emerge from the 2005 Tory leadership contest, open to all Tory members, was that fewer than 200 000 people voted — this in a party that once had almost 3 million members. In the Liberal Democrat leadership contest of 2006, a mere 52 036 votes were recorded.
- *De-energised party members.* Drawing upon the research of Professor Patrick Seyd, POWER reported that today's party members were not only fewer in number, but also more lacklustre. Only 11% of Conservative members had attended more than five party meetings in a year, while the

figure for Labour members was 18% (61% of Labour members had not attended a single meeting in a year).

Having illustrated the unpopularity of political parties, POWER then sought to explain it:

- *Class dealignment.* The two main parties once drew their support from two fairly homogeneous social classes, reflecting an economy based on manufacturing industry. That economy has all but disappeared, with society becoming more diverse as a result. Put simply, voters no longer identify so easily with either the working class or the middle class, and therefore feel less attached to a party system still dominated by two class-based parties.
- *A more sophisticated electorate.* More than ever, voters are now forming independent views that do not conform to any party package. When forming those views, voters no longer take their cue from the policies of one particular party. Indeed, they may develop a range of views that cut across party positions.
- *'All the same'.* Voters are aware that, in recent years, the main parties' policies have converged, limiting any substantial choice between them. As POWER observed, 'The main parties are guided by the search for votes from the centre ground rather than any deeply-held values'. The continuities between New Labour and the previous Tory government, in areas such as education and privatisation, have only fuelled this impression.
- *Undemocratic party structures.* Parties have a reputation for being 'top-down' organisations, driven by 'control freak' leaders who ignore the views of ordinary party members. As such, they seem out of tune with our 'karaoke culture', in which ordinary citizens are increasingly restless for influence. More than any other party, New Labour has upheld this view — with its policy directions (in such areas as foreign policy) sidelining party members. In the words of one Labour activist: 'The power we have locally is negligible, and I don't think we have any say over national policy at all.'
- *Party funding.* Linked to 'elitist' party structures is the way the main parties raise money. Both the Labour and Conservative parties have become increasingly reliant upon large donations from wealthy individuals — members' subscriptions now constitute only 10% of Conservative revenue and 8% of Labour revenue — thus giving the impression that parties are in the pockets of vested interests.
- *Improper conduct.* Party funding has given rise to a widely held view that parties are somewhat corrupt — an impression fortified by the 'cash for peerages' scandal of 2006. Since the 1990s, both the main parties have been embroiled in various 'sleaze' allegations, calling their integrity into question. Although POWER did not 'name and shame', it seems fair to assume that the scandals affecting Jeffrey Archer, David Blunkett and (since POWER was published) John Prescott are obvious examples. However, the report was keen to stress that the behaviour of individual politicians was not the main reason for the discrediting of political parties: 'The problem is systemic, not personal.'

Why is the political system seen as unaccountable?

POWER cited the growth of a 'quiet authoritarianism' in the way that we are governed, noting a dangerous irony: 'Just as the country's citizens expect more influence over the decisions that affect them, the decision-makers themselves seem more remote and less accountable.' The report gave a number of examples:

- *Inadequate House of Commons scrutiny.* Despite growing backbench dissent, New Labour's substantial majorities have made the Commons seem a rubber stamp, in that party discipline is used to enforce policies lacking public confidence — student tuition fees, foundation hospitals and trust schools being arguable examples.
- *Undemocratic second chamber.* Despite reform of the House of Lords in 1998, it remains an unelected body, disconnected from formal accountability to the public. That half the legislature is so obviously undemocratic seems anomalous, given the situation in other democracies and the increasingly democratic tone of our own culture.
- *Unrepresentative representatives.* The disconnection between people and parliament is heightened by MPs' backgrounds. If parliament were to reflect the make-up of society, there should be about 320 women MPs, including 50 from ethnic minorities; instead, the current figures are 128 and 15. Furthermore, a third of MPs were educated at private schools — even though 92% of the electorate was not.
- *Disproportionate representation.* Owing to the anomalies of the first-past-the-post electoral system, there seems only a tenuous link between voting behaviour and the composition of the Commons. For example, Labour secured only 35% of the votes in 2005, but gained 55% of seats, while Liberal Democrats had only 11% of seats, despite gaining 22% of the votes. These figures, POWER implied, further undermine voters' respect for parliamentary government and foment disrespect for both law makers and law enforcers.
- *From town hall to Whitehall.* Since the 1970s, local government has lost many powers to central government in London. In education, for example, powers once wielded by local education authorities — such as curriculum development and teachers' salaries — have passed into the hands of Whitehall. New Labour's attempts to correct this (via reforms such as the introduction of city academies) have often empowered business rather than elected officials.

Are new democratic forces sidelined?

POWER tried to show that, despite signs of disenchantment with representative democracy, other forms of democratic activity are flourishing; 'political apathy', it claims, is a myth. This can be shown in a number of ways:

- *An exponential growth of pressure groups.* Since the 1980s, there has been a phenomenal expansion of pressure-group activity, particularly since the advent of the internet. Some groups have also seen a huge rise in membership: having had 30 000 members in 1981, Greenpeace now has 221 000; the Royal Society for the Protection of Birds, with a membership of 98 000 in 1971, now has over 1 million members.

- *A growing interest in ad hoc campaigns.* The public seems especially keen on campaigns that arise to meet current problems. In 2002, for example, over half a million took part in various Countryside Alliance demonstrations, responding to the government's proposed ban on fox hunting. In 2003, after the start of the Iraq war, 1.5 million took part in Stop the War's marches and rallies. In 2005, the Live 8 concert in Hyde Park (ahead of the G8 summit) attracted over 150 000 people. POWER also noted that, in 2004, an estimated 42% of voters had signed some sort of petition during the previous 2 years — double the figure suggested for 1974.

As POWER pointed out, it is not the case that those involved in this 'informal' democracy are the same as those still voting. In its poll of abstainers from the 2005 general election, 37% said that they were members of a pressure group, campaign, community group or charitable organisation.

Yet, according to the report, these burgeoning democratic forces are not being harnessed by the state. Indeed, since 2001, the Blair government has seemed to glory in the idea of strong, autocratic government that defies 'short-term' public opinion. Its 1997 promise of more direct democracy, via referendum, seems to have been repealed — hastened perhaps by the 2004 referendum on regional government in the northeast, which left the government rejected and embarrassed.

However, as POWER noted, it is wrong to single out this government when explaining why the growing democratic culture, as illustrated above, has not yet affected the institutions of state. Those institutions, it argued, are deeply embedded in a pre-democratic culture of unitary power, secrecy and patronage, compounded by the absence of a modern, codified constitution.

What were POWER's proposals?

The POWER commissioners stressed that the reforms they proposed were not incremental; nor could they be 'cherry-picked'. If the reforms were to be effective, they would have to be introduced together as part of a general overhaul of our political system — one that would tie it to the new character of our culture and society.

POWER also stressed that it was no enemy of representative democracy: it rejected 'utopian' ideas of a mainly 'direct' democracy (involving, for example, referenda on most issues), but re-asserted the importance of a healthy parliamentary system, supported by popular political parties. It also defended the rationale of political parties, highlighting their 'unique and vital' role in aggregating and reconciling society's diverse interests. Yet it still asserted that, if representative democracy were to survive, it needed urgent surgery. POWER duly sought solutions to the four key problems that it had highlighted.

How can turnout be improved?

POWER recommended the following:

- *Proportional representation (PR) for Westminster.* The commissioners recorded that, in the 164 countries using PR, turnout was, on average, 10% higher than in the UK, with the decline in turnout less severe. POWER emphatically rejected the 'closed list' form of PR, noting that it allowed voters to choose only parties, not candidates, and that it placed too much power in the hands of party managers. But POWER strongly advocated single transferable vote (STV), for the following reasons:
  - It would allow voters to choose between a party's candidates and reject certain 'wings' of a party.
  - It would encourage parties to field candidates from a wider range of backgrounds.
  - It would give independents and smaller parties a chance of election, thus giving voters a wider choice of credible candidates.
  - It would reduce the number of 'safe' seats and thus make more voters feel that their votes counted.
- *Reduction of voting/candidate age to 16.* POWER was impressed by the high number of young people involved in various campaigns (such as Make Poverty History). It also thought it anomalous that while many rights and duties were accorded 16–18-year-olds — such as paying tax in certain circumstances — the right to vote was denied. It also suggested that more young people might vote if more young candidates were allowed, and it duly recommended that the minimum age for candidates should also be 16.
- *Improved political education in schools.* This was seen as an accompaniment to lowering the voting age, but was also thought helpful in terms of raising political interest beyond school and college.
- *Possibility of more referenda/single-issue ballots.* People might be more inclined to vote if they did not have to endorse everything a party stood for, and would reflect the growing interest in single-issue politics. A growing culture of referenda would allow voters to think that, on certain specific issues, they could later instruct or correct the party that they were about to vote for.

Although POWER thought that more women and black candidates would increase turnout, it rejected positive discrimination (e.g. all-women shortlists) during candidate selection. Instead, it believed that sexual and racial imbalance would be rectified 'naturally' through the wider range of candidates implicit in STV.

POWER also rejected the idea of voting via text, telephone or e-mail — even though 44% of abstainers said that this would make them more likely to vote. As well as increasing the likelihood of fraud, these schemes were said to lack the 'poignancy' of a visit to the polling station and were unlikely to remind people of the seriousness of elections.

How can parties be made more popular?

POWER recommended the following:

- *Single transferable vote.* As already implied, this type of electoral reform would encourage parties to choose a wider range of candidates who would be more likely to connect with voters. The reduction of 'safe' seats would also make parties less complacent and insensitive in many constituencies.
- *More democratic party structures.* If parties were to shed their reputation for aloofness, they would have to give their members more obvious influence over candidate selection, leader selection and policy formation. US-style 'primary' elections, in which candidates are chosen by voters as well as party members, would be one way of making party business less obscure to ordinary voters.
- *Reform of party funding.* To make party finance less plutocratic, there would be a cap (of £10 000) on any individual's donation to a political party. There would also be increased state funding, but in a way linked to public support — a party would get £3 of public money for every voter who indicated (on the ballot paper at a general election) that he or she wished this to happen.

How can the political system be made more accountable?

POWER recommended the following:

- *Enhancing the House of Commons in relation to government.* The report suggested a strengthening of select committees, more opportunities for back-benchers to initiate legislation and a limitation on the power of whips — all underpinned by a new 'concordat' between executive and legislature, pinpointing who does what.
- *Democratising the House of Lords.* Seventy per cent of its members would be elected for a period of three parliaments, with only a third of them elected at each general election (thus avoiding two Houses with much the same political colour).
- *The restoration of local government.* This would be accomplished partly by a 'concordat' between central and local government — giving the latter certain fixed powers — and a new system of local government finance, whereby councils would raise most of their own revenue through local taxation.
- *A formal check upon government involvement in supranational bodies.* To address the effects of globalisation upon our democracy, an all-parliament select committee was proposed to scrutinise ministers' actions in the 400 000 or so intergovernmental conferences held each year.
- *MPs to regularise their links with their constituents.* This would be done chiefly via annual reports, debated within AGMs open to all their constituents.

How can society's new democratic forces be harnessed?

POWER recommended the following:

- *More direct democracy.* Legislative proposals backed by 1% of the electorate in a petition would be debated and voted on by parliament. If parliament rejected such a proposal, and it were then backed by a further petition, signed by a further 1% of voters, it would be subject to a nationwide referendum. If backed by a majority of voters, on a turnout of at least 60%, the proposal would be legalised automatically (though such initiatives would not be allowed in respect of fiscal and budgetary matters).

- *Contact with pressure groups formalised*. Ministers would be formally obliged to consult affected pressure groups and keep a record of the discussions that took place. New pressure groups could formally apply for inclusion in such consultations.
- *Democratisation of broadcasting*. Television and radio executives would be required to broaden their consultation strategies and widen the opportunities for citizens and pressure groups to access the media.
- *'Democracy Hubs'*. In each local authority, there would be a Democracy Hub — a type of citizens' advice bureau, offering guidance through the political system for groups and individuals seeking change.

Conclusion: far-sighted report or liberal twaddle?

The POWER inquiry's report is essential reading for anyone interested in the health of UK democracy. It is well written, well researched and well presented. However, it appears to overlook a number of points that seem relevant to explaining the current problems of representative democracy in the UK.

Since the end of the Cold War, and the subsequent adjustments made by those on the left of politics, the 'big picture' of politics has been largely resolved. We no longer argue as much over the fundamentals of society (capitalism or socialism? private enterprise or state control?) and generally accept the 'social market' character of society — one marked by a mixture of expanding private enterprise, consumer choice, expansive public services and high levels of taxation.

Yet it was these 'fundamentalist' arguments — and the prospect of profound change — that once gave party politics, elections and representative democracy such urgency. For many Labour voters, there seemed a real prospect of significant change to society, while for many Tory voters, there was a strong wish to resist it. The result of general elections thus had a crucial bearing upon the future of the country — as those of 1945 and 1979 demonstrated.

But this ideological type of politics has now been replaced by something more managerial and 'particularistic'. It is a development that does much to explain the growth of pressure groups and the declining popularity of the 'generalistic' politics embodied by parties and the parliamentary system.

POWER lamented the lack of substantial choice between the policies offered by the main parties, but it ignored the fact that *consensus politics seems to reflect a consensus among voters*. Voters are now generally agreed on a society that mixes private enterprise, extensive public services and the relatively high public spending that goes with it. In this respect, we may be getting the representative politics we deserve — and subconsciously want.

With this in mind, the proposals put forward by POWER seem only to scratch the surface. It will take more than 'Democracy Hubs' and 'concordats' to re-create the levels of interest in representative politics maintained until the 1990s. On the other hand, a perilous economic recession, plus some tangible threat to the nature of society, could generate interest. Neither of these situations seems likely for a while — and few would hasten their arrival.

Summary

- The POWER Commission thinks that UK democracy is in crisis.
- It thinks that representative democracy is suffering from huge public disengagement.
- It thinks that the UK political system is out of tune with society.
- It rejects the idea that British citizens are politically disinterested.
- It believes that representative democracy should be updated and reformed.
- It believes that representative democracy should be supplemented, rather than replaced by, a largely 'direct' democratic system.

Chapter 7

Lords reform: the beginning of the end?

About this chapter

In the Queen's speech on 15 November 2006, the government said that it would 'bring forward proposals' for reform of the House of Lords but did not promise a vote during the current session of parliament. The Queen said that the government would continue with its reform programme and would 'work to build a consensus on reform of the House of Lords'. Jack Straw stated that he was in 'intensive talks' with the other main parties and promised a free vote on any proposed make-up of a reformed House of Lords. This chapter will answer the following questions:

- What proposals for Lords reform emerged in 2006?
- How do such proposals deal with the controversial issue of election and/or appointment to a reformed upper House?
- How, and why, has Lords reform come back onto the political agenda in 2006?
- What is the Legislative and Regulatory Reform Bill and how comfortably did it sit with Labour's 2005 manifesto commitment to improve Commons scrutiny?

What proposals for Lords reform were being mooted by the end of 2006?

The leader of the Commons, Jack Straw, set out his thoughts in a leaked agenda for the cross-party working group on House of Lords reform, dated 12 October 2006. This document addressed many of the issues that had undermined earlier efforts at reaching a cross-party consensus on the issue (see Box 7.1).

Box 7.1 An agenda for cross-party discussions

(1) Principles of composition

- Does reformed chamber complement or duplicate House of Commons?
- If complement, key principles:
  - (a) party balance
  - (b) crossbench/independent members
  - (c) Church of England bishops and other religious representatives
  - (d) gender balance, representation of ethnic minority members; regional representation

(2) Membership of the House

- Balance between elected and appointed

(3) Other matters

(a) size of chamber

(b) terms of membership

(c) prime minister's ability directly to make appointments

(d) payment and resourcing of members

Source: *Agenda — Cross Party Working Group on House of Lords Reform*, 12 October 2006.

What solutions did Straw's paper offer in each of the areas identified for discussion?

Should the new chamber duplicate or complement the House of Commons?

As Meghnad Desai of the House of Lords noted in his letter to the *Guardian* on 25 October 2006:

> The principle obstacle to House of Lords reform is, and always has been, the House of Commons. It arises from the fact that among all countries with bicameral parliaments, ours is the only one which presumes primacy of one house over the other…While the incumbent elected house exercises a veto on the creation of another elected chamber, we are all condemned to drift.

The first section of Straw's discussion paper dealt with this issue under the broad heading 'Principles of Composition'. For the leader of the House, and many others, the key issue was whether the chamber replacing the current House of Lords should duplicate the Commons in terms of composition and party balance, or whether it should instead be composed in such a way as to complement the lower house, as is the case under the present arrangements. This issue of composition is, of course, directly related to the issues of power and the Commons' primacy alluded to in Desai's letter. This is because a second chamber that mirrored the first in terms of composition might reasonably argue that it had as much of a mandate to legislate as the Commons. Issues of composition are, therefore, inextricably linked to those of role and powers, as are issues such as the correct blend between elected and appointed members, the length of members' terms and the arrangements under which members might be elected — all issues to which we will be returning later in this chapter.

Straw's paper recognised that in the modern era the Lords had served to complement the 'primary chamber' in terms of composition and powers. Though 'there are examples of second chambers that effectively duplicate the functions of their primary chamber (e.g. the Italian senate)', Straw argued, 'second chambers [more often] provide a complementary function [that] is usually reflected in both powers and composition'. The Lords' role in recent times has, therefore, been to revise and scrutinise legislation originating in the Commons, rather than to become a rival institution. Accepting that this should in principle remain the case, the discussion paper went on to identify principles of composition that might allow the second chamber to perform this complementary function more effectively.

Assuming that it should complement the Commons, what principles should underpin the composition of the House of Lords?

(1) Party balance. The in-built Tory majority in the Lords had almost vanished by the time *Annual Survey 2006* was written. The abolition of all but 92 of the hereditary peers and the appointment of a disproportionate number of Labour life peers had created virtual parity between Labour and the Conservatives. Indeed, by July 2006, Labour peers marginally outnumbered those on the Conservative benches (see Table 7.1). Straw's cross-party discussion paper recognised the way in which the absence of single-party control in the second chamber had allowed the House of Lords to be more effective in its scrutiny of government proposals. The 'hung' nature of the second chamber and the presence of so many crossbenchers had also helped to provide a 'clear distinction' between the two houses of parliament. As a result of such benefits, the paper concluded that 'this essential principle should remain in a reformed House and no single party, no matter how big its majority in the House of Commons, should command an overall majority in the House of Lords'.

Party	Peers
Crossbench/bishops/other	239
Labour	213
Conservative	210
Liberal Democrats	79
Total	*741*

Source: House of Lords Information Office.

Table 7.1 Membership of the Lords, July 2006

(2) Crossbench/independent members. The presence of so many crossbenchers in the House of Lords has been crucial in determining its distinctive character. In 2000, the Wakeham Report — which looked to determine the future course of Lords reform in the wake of the House of Lords Act 1999 — advised that the easiest way of preventing a single party from having a majority in the reformed chamber would be to require 20% of members to be crossbenchers. Straw appeared to accept broadly such a proposal in October 2006, arguing that the contribution made by crossbenchers under the present arrangements had been considerable — not least as a result of the 'wealth of experience' that such members often brought to the chamber.

(3) Church of England bishops and other religious representatives. Senior bishops have sat in the House of Lords by right since its creation. Though Straw's paper recognised the contribution of such members to the work of the chamber, it suggested that the number of places reserved for the clergy may reasonably be reduced from 26 to 16 in the reformed chamber. Furthermore, a bishop's place should depend on genuine interest in contributing to the work of the house rather than just on seniority in the Church, as is currently the case. The paper also suggested that a new Lords Appointments Commission could be required to try to select some members representing other religious faiths, so as to recognise that the UK is now a multicultural and multi-faith society.

(4) Gender balance: representation of ethnic minority members. In the same way that the Appointments Commission might be required to ensure that the major faiths are represented in the reformed house, it was envisaged that it should also endeavour to achieve better balance in terms of gender and race.

(5) Regional representation. In many Western countries, the second chamber plays a role in providing enhanced regional and/or local representation. In the USA, for example, the Senate gives equal representation to each state (two members) regardless of state population. Prior to the Seventeenth Amendment in 1913, such individuals were chosen by their state legislatures as opposed to being directly elected by the citizens of each state. Under the German federal system, the Bundesrat performs a similar function, as does the second chamber (the senate) in France and in Ireland. Under Straw's proposals, the second chamber would represent the regions in a similar manner, regardless of the method of composition eventually agreed. Though members would not have constituencies and would not, therefore, be rivals to their counterparts in the Commons, those serving in the reformed house would be expected to perform a broader representative function in respect of their assigned regions.

How big should the reformed house be and should it comprise members who are elected, appointed or a combination of the two?

In July 2006, the UK Parliament comprised 1387 members: 741 peers and 646 in the House of Commons. This is significantly more than the number of members in most comparable Western legislatures. In the USA, for example, which has a population five times that of the UK, there are only 535 members in Congress — 435 in the House of Representatives and 100 in the Senate. Many have argued that this disparity between the size of the UK Parliament and comparable Western legislatures, allied to the sheer physical limitations presented by the buildings that comprise the Palace of Westminster, makes the case for a reduction in the size of the UK legislature compelling. Under the proposals advanced by Straw in October 2006, the reformed second chamber would, therefore, be capped at 450 members.

A second and perhaps more crucial issue that needs to be addressed is precisely where to strike the balance between the numbers of elected and appointed members. In its 2001 white paper on completing Lords reform, the government had envisaged a chamber in which around 20% of the 600 members would be elected. The two main opposition parties, in contrast, were united in calling for a smaller 'senate' of around 300 members, with 80% elected. As we saw in *Annual Survey 2006*, it was this lack of a consensus over precisely where to strike the balance between the elected and appointed elements of the reformed house that ultimately led to the rejection of all eight models — ranging from a totally elected chamber to its outright abolition — in 2003.

By October 2006, however, broad agreement appeared to be emerging on this issue. It was said that the prime minister had dropped his preference for a largely appointed chamber, having been convinced by the arguments of those who opposed such a settlement. Though stopping short of accepting the recommendations of the POWER inquiry (see Box 7.2), Straw's proposals appeared to offer the prospect of a chamber that was made up of elected and appointed members in equal number (50:50). The discussion paper also provided for a system of election that would ensure that the chamber retained a character very different from that of the Commons. First, Lords elections would not all take place at the same time. Instead, the elected element of the House of Lords would be chosen in three separate cohorts over the next three parliamentary terms. This system of staggered elections (see Box 7.3) would virtually mirror that in place for elections to the US Senate. Second, those elected to the new chamber, like their appointed counterparts, would sit for a single, non-renewable period equal to three Commons terms (around 12 years). Third, elected members of the new house might be chosen under a more proportional regional party list system. This would both address the desire to provide an element of regional representation (as outlined above) and make it less likely that a single party would hold a majority in the reformed chamber. Such elections might operate using the same regions as those used in UK elections to the European Parliament, although the list system might be partially 'open', so as to allow voters the opportunity to express a preference for individual candidates on a given party's list, as opposed to simply voting for the party.

> ### Box 7.2 The POWER report and Lords reform
>
> 'Seventy per cent of the members of the House of Lords should be elected by a "responsive electoral system" — and not on a closed party list system — for three parliamentary terms. To ensure that this part of the legislature is not comprised of career politicians with no experience outside politics, candidates should be at least 40 years of age.'
>
> Source: adapted from *Power to the People* (the report of POWER, an independent inquiry into Britain's democracy), February 2006.

> **Box 7.3** **Staggering Lords elections**
>
> 'In a reformed House of the kind discussed in this paper, the advantages of the current life-membership system could be retained to a significant extent if members were, say, to serve three parliament terms equating to a minimum of 12 years, with no provision for re-appointment or re-election. Making terms non-renewable should help to guarantee their independence. Staggering the process over three election cycles allows a more manageable process, whilst keeping the valuable continuity of membership and ensuring the House is regularly refreshed with new talent.'
>
> Source: *Agenda — Cross Party Working Group on House of Lords Reform* (paragraph 55), 12 October 2006.

Under Straw's proposals, appointed peers would be chosen by a new, nine-member statutory Appointments Commission that would be charged with addressing the need for racial, religious and gender balance outlined earlier. The commission would be funded by, and accountable to, parliament, rather than to ministers. Each of the three main parties would be able to nominate one member of this commission, with one coming from the crossbenches and a further five — one of whom would be the chair of the commission — selected independently by parliament.

With members of the reformed chamber also prevented from seeking re-election or re-appointment, and those chosen receiving a full salary as opposed to the daily allowance available at present, it was hoped that the reformed house would become an even more effective legislative chamber than it is at present.

Thus, by October 2006, there appeared to be a clear road map for the completion of the programme of Lords reform started in Labour's first term (see Box 7.4). With Lord McNally, the Liberal Democrats' leader in the House of Lords, describing the proposals as 'the most serious and well thought

> **Box 7.4** **The new agenda on Lords reform: a summary**
>
> - A reduction in the size of the second chamber from over 700 members to 450.
> - No party to hold a majority in the new chamber.
> - A 50:50 split between elected and unelected members.
> - Elected members to be elected in three cohorts over the three general elections (i.e. around 80 per election), under a partially open regional list system.
> - Appointed members to be chosen by a new statutory independent Appointments Commission.
> - New members to serve a non-renewable fixed term of around three parliamentary sessions, or 12 years.
> - Members to work full time and be salaried.

through contribution from the government since 1998', and the Conservatives offering guarded support for at least some of the leaked proposals, significant progress appeared closer than it had been for some time.

One significant question remains, however: how had the issue of Lords reform suddenly found its way back onto the political agenda, when progress appeared so far off in January 2006 (see Box 7.5)?

Box 7.5 **Prospects for Lords reform**

'Lords reform remains on the government's agenda, but it is hard to see how this is going to progress. As reported in the September 2005 *Monitor*, the Queen's Speech didn't promise a bill immediately, and the first task was to establish a new parliamentary joint committee. However, even this has not occurred, due to disagreement between the parties about its terms of reference.'

Source: *Monitor* (the newsletter of the Constitution Unit), January 2006.

How had Lords reform found its way back onto the political agenda?

The new impetus towards completing Lords reform was clearly not prompted, in the first instance at least, by changing public opinion. In a poll produced for *The Times* in April 2006, for example, public confusion appeared to reign, with 75% agreeing that the House of Lords 'should remain a mainly appointed house' in order to retain its independence and expertise, and 72% believing that 'at least half of the members of the Lords should be elected' in order to ensure that the upper chamber has 'democratic legitimacy'.

Even though there was confusion over what precisely should be done, there was a growing consensus that the matter could not simply be left alone. What factors prompted such a desire for change?

The need to complete the programme

By the end of 2006, the government was coming under increased pressure to complete the programme of Lords reform that it had initiated in 1998 (see Box 7.6). Though some of this criticism was clearly linked to the broader political context (see later in this chapter), many had come to regard the situation as untenable at best, and often wholly risible. The same could be said of the position of the remaining 92 hereditaries, chosen by their peers in 1999 to continue sitting in the transitional House of Lords. First, there has been the bizarre spectacle of the elections periodically held to fill vacancies among the 92 (see Box 7.7). Second, there is the fact that the remaining hereditaries appear to be working far harder than regular life peers or the much heralded 'people's peers' first appointed in May 2000 (see Box 7.8).

Such realities have clearly fuelled Labour's desire to complete a programme that has remained stalled since all eight models for Lords reform were rejected in 2003.

The political context

Aside from Labour's natural desire to complete the programme of Lords reform, the changing political context also played a part in bringing the issue back onto the agenda in 2006. The government's problems with foreign affairs inevitably saw it refocusing its efforts on the domestic front. The sense that time might be running out for New Labour — particularly in light of the

Conservatives' resurgence in the polls under the leadership of David Cameron — also concentrated minds.

The treatment meted out to the government in the Lords since 2001 (see Figure 7.1) may also have played a part in bringing the issue of Lords reform to the fore. In the spring of 2006 a series of articles in the quality press suggested that the government was ready to limit the powers of an upper house that had proved a considerable obstacle to New Labour over issues as wide-ranging as hunting, terrorism, ID cards and education reform. In March 2006 the *Independent* reported that the Salisbury Doctrine (according to which the House of Lords should not reject at second or third reading government bills brought from the House of Commons for which the government has a mandate from the nation) was to be given statutory force in response to the suggestion that peers might seek to defy the long-standing convention and block manifesto pledges. By May, the *Guardian* was suggesting that Tony Blair was bringing in former Labour cabinet minister Jack (now Lord) Cunningham to head a committee with a remit to 'curb Lords powers', after the prime minister had 'torn up' plans under which changes in the power of the Lords would accompany the move to a part-elected second chamber. However, the prime minister's efforts to limit the House of Lords' powers without making concessions on the composition of the house were thwarted by a third crucial factor — the criminal investigation into Labour's alleged sale of peerages.

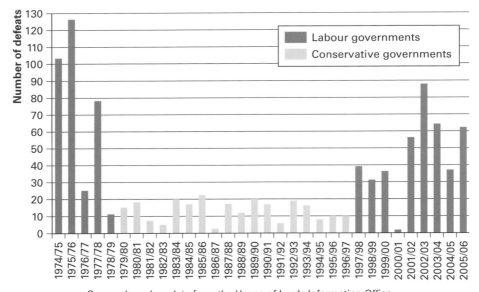

Source: based on data from the House of Lords Information Office.

Note: figures for 2005/06 are as of 2 November 2006

Figure 7.1 Government defeats in the House of Lords, 1974/75 to 2005/06

The fallout from the 'loans for peerages' scandal

Issues of party funding are dealt with elsewhere in this book (see Chapter 5), but we must mention here the 'loans for peerages' scandal. Indeed, we should not underestimate the part that it played in putting Lords reform back on the agenda.

Before the scandal, Labour appeared more intent on reducing the Lords' power to delay government bills than on completing the reform of the composition of the upper chamber that began in 1998 (see Box 7.9). With the emerging scandal over Labour's alleged 'sale' of peerages, it was now clearly desirable for the government to distance itself quickly from the appointments process. This renewed willingness to discuss issues of the House of Lords' composition, as well as its powers, broke the inter-party deadlock over Lords reform that had existed in the early part of the year.

Box 7.9 **Cash for peerages and Lords reform**

'The "cash for peerages" row reignited debates about reform of the House of Lords. A proposed joint committee to consider reform options had been delayed due to Liberal Democrat objections to its remit, which the government proposed should cover only powers and conventions rather than composition. To generate movement, the government backed down and a new committee will now consider all related issues.'

Source: *Monitor*, May 2006.

What was the government trying to achieve in introducing the Legislative and Regulatory Reform Bill?

What would the original Bill have done?

Under the Regulatory Reform Act 2001, the government was permitted to propose so-called regulatory reform orders. These orders allowed ministers to amend statute through 'delegated', rather than further 'primary', legislation, with a view to removing excessive regulatory burdens on businesses and other bodies. The Legislative and Regulatory Reform Bill (LRRB) sought to extend significantly such powers. Cabinet Office Minister Jim Murphy argued that the proposed changes would thereby 'help deliver billions of pounds in savings for the UK economy through reducing the regulatory burden imposed on businesses, and ease the burden imposed by redundant and out-of-date bureaucracy on nurses, doctors, police and charity workers'.

Why did the LRRB provoke such opposition?

While such aims may indeed be commendable, the far-reaching powers outlined in Part 1 of the Bill (see Box 7.10) faced considerable opposition both within parliament (see Box 7.11) and among interested parties outside of the legislature, such as the Constitution Unit.

Box 7.10 The 'Abolition of Parliament Bill'

'The *Legislative and Regulatory Reform Bill 2005–06* extends the scope of the powers available to Ministers to amend statute law by Order and at the same time relaxes the constraints of parliamentary scrutiny on the Order making process...The wide-ranging power in Part 1 of the Bill potentially allows ministers to amend, repeal or replace any legislation, although the Government has committed itself to not using the procedure to deliver "highly political measures".'

Source: Richard Kelly and Vincent Keter, *The Legislative and Regulatory Reform Bill 2005–06*, House of Commons Research Paper 06/06, 6 February 2006.

Box 7.11 Opposition to the LRRB

'The House of Lords Constitution Committee expressed a fear the [LRRB] could "markedly alter the respective and long-established roles of Ministers and Parliament in the legislative process", while in the Commons, the Regulatory Reform Committee thought the Bill "the most constitutionally significant Bill that has been brought before Parliament for some years". The Public Administration Select Committee added its criticism.'

Source: *Monitor*, May 2006.

The central criticism of the Bill was that while it was purported to be a way of cutting unnecessary regulation (the oft-mentioned 'red tape'), it was in fact framed so widely as to give ministers the power to amend any bill, even if there was no subsequent cost benefit in terms of reducing bureaucracy. It was argued that ministers would be able to bring about significant constitutional changes, including making changes to the Parliament Act, without the need for further primary legislation. It was these powers that earned the LRRB the nickname of the 'Parliament Scrutiny (Abolition) Bill' and the 'Abolition of Parliament Bill'.

Such a measure appeared strangely at odds with Labour's own 2005 Manifesto pledge to 'improve the effectiveness of Commons scrutiny', the possible implications of which were discussed in *Annual Survey 2006*. The LRRB also appeared to be out of step with the kinds of ideas on Commons reform being floated by organisations such as the POWER inquiry in 2006 (see Box 7.12 and Chapter 6).

Box 7.12 The POWER report on parliamentary scrutiny

(1) A Concordat should be drawn up between Executive and Parliament indicating where key powers lie and providing significant powers of scrutiny and initiation for Parliament.

(2) Select Committees should be given independence and enhanced powers, including the power to scrutinise and veto key government appointments and to subpoena witnesses to appear and testify before them. This should include proper resourcing so that Committees can fulfil their remit effectively. The specialist committees in the upper house should have the power to co-opt people from outside the legislature who have singular expertise, such as specialist scientists, when considering complex areas of legislation or policy.

(3) Limits should be placed on the power of the whips.

(4) Parliament should have greater powers to initiate legislation, to launch public inquiries and to act on public petitions.

Source: *Power to the People*, February 2006.

In the face of such widespread opposition to the Bill, the government backed down, with a series of concessions and speeches designed to reduce opposition. By 13 April 2006, the *Guardian* was reporting that Cabinet Office Minister Jim Murphy was looking to build bridges with the Bill's opponents. 'It wasn't and isn't our intention to do the sort of things that to some extent have been suggested,' he maintained. 'There's been hyperbole and ridiculous claims…This Bill is about regulations; it has never been about [changing] the constitution.' On 4 May, Murphy's words were given form with the publication of amendments that allow committees in both the Commons and the Lords a statutory power of veto over ministers proposing a legislative change under the Act, provided that they use this veto within 40 days. There was also the requirement that any changes made by ministers under the powers given to them in the Bill would serve the primary purpose of reducing the regulatory burden.

Such far-reaching concessions were, not surprisingly, welcomed by those who had opposed the Bill in its original form (see Box 7.13). Further concessions on 10 May — which included preventing ministers from using the LRRB to amend the Human Rights Act 1998 — proved sufficient for the Bill to receive its third reading in the Commons on 16 May. The Bill then moved to the

Box 7.13 Opposition parties welcome concessions

'Oliver Heald, shadow constitutional affairs secretary, told Radio 4's *Today* programme: "It is a significant climbdown by the government. The amendments will say you can only use this power for deregulation and so the central issue of this order-making power has been resolved." As for the Liberal Democrats, Simon Hughes stated that the amendments "certainly made the risk of this legislation much less", though he also said that further change was needed.'

Source: adapted from Will Woodward, 'Climbdown over Bill critics claimed was a move to bypass parliament', *Guardian*, 5 May 2006.

Lords, where it received its third reading on 2 November and was sent back to the Commons with amendments. The Bill eventually received royal assent on 8 November.

Conclusion: where is parliament going?

The government's failure to complete its programme of Lords reform, its increasingly strained relations with the upper house, and the perception — however misplaced — that measures such as the LRRB were part of a broader desire to bypass the legislature, have hardly served to enhance public confidence in parliament. Indeed, such realities have contributed to an impression that parliament is increasingly weak and ineffectual (see Box 7.14).

Box 7.14   Parliament's end-of-term report

'If politics really were a sport, the last year at Westminster would be remembered as a vintage season. Since it is not, MPs will drift off tomorrow into a 77-day recess with barely a cheer for their efforts. Jaded by the government and the parliamentary culture that produced it, voters are becoming immune to the suggestion that anything about the political system works.

Yet for every Lord Levy there is a Lady Williams, and for every backbench drone there is an MP doing their job well. Writing off the Commons as tired and timid has become a staple of journalism, but it is unfair as a caricature of the last year, which has been one of the more effective parliamentary spells of modern times.

The Lords, meanwhile, routinely challenged the government — 53 defeats since October.'

Source: adapted from 'Parliament — end of term report', *Guardian*, 24 July 2006.

In fact, this is not the case:
- First, as we have seen (Figure 7.1), the Lords have been as willing to defeat the government over the last 5 years as they have been at any time since the mid-1970s.
- Second, the changes proposed in the cross-party agenda on Lords reform, leaked in October, offer the prospect of a reformed house with greater legitimacy. Such a house may feel even more justified in and committed to the task of holding the Commons to account.
- Third, though the LRRB in its original form may have had the effect of limiting parliamentary scrutiny, we should remember that it was not passed in its original form, owing to the level of parliamentary opposition.

The reality is that parliament is working far more effectively than most commentators are prepared to admit. The House of Lords — supposedly stuffed with 'Tony's cronies' — has acted as an extremely effective check on government ambitions. The Commons — dominated, we are told, by New

Labour 'poodles' — has, in reality, become increasingly rebellious, as Philip Cowley of the University of Nottingham noted in his lectures (see Box 7.15), in print and on his website (**www.revolts.co.uk**).

| Box 7.15 | **The rise of parliament** |

MPs are now more likely:

- to come from their constituency
- to live in their constituency
- to have staffed offices in their constituency
- to spend time in the constituency
- to receive mail (and e-mails)
- to be writing to their constituents

- to defy the whip:
  - majority of 60+, but four defeats
  - free votes and other retreats
  - rebellions run at 27% in first session
  - other victories by single figures
  - other victories thanks to Conservative support

Source: adapted from a presentation given by Philip Cowley at the Politics Association Annual Conference, September 2006.

Summary

- Further Lords reform appeared far more likely at the end of 2006 than it had at the beginning of the year.
- This renewed enthusiasm for reform was in part born of a widely felt desire to finish a job that had been started almost a decade before.
- The call for Lords reform was further fuelled by the growing furore over the 'loans for peerages' scandal, as well as the broader political context.
- The Legislative and Regulatory Reform Bill was supposed to make it easier for ministers to remove unnecessary red tape without having to resort to primary legislation.
- However, the bill was widely seen as an attempt to undermine parliamentary control and empower ministers to make significant — possibly even constitutional — changes without proper parliamentary scrutiny. Critics dubbed it the 'Abolition of Parliament Bill'.
- The likelihood that the bill would be defeated by its opponents in parliament prompted the government to make sweeping concessions.
- Though some in the popular press persist in portraying MPs and peers as helpless (even spineless) in the face of a rampant executive, many informed commentators regard the current parliament as the most effective in a generation.

Chapter 8

The Human Rights Act: why so controversial?

About this chapter

In Chapter 12 of *Annual Survey 2006* we considered the ways in which the implementation of the Human Rights Act 1998 and the Freedom of Information Act 2000 had contributed to the emergence of a new rights culture in the UK. Since then, however, the first of these measures has become the subject of intense controversy, with both senior government ministers — including Home Secretary John Reid — and the Official Opposition arguing that the way in which the Act has been applied serves to undermine the efforts of the security services and other law-enforcement agencies.

This chapter examines some of the proposals for change brought forward in recent months, before considering why it is that the Human Rights Act (HRA) has been subject to such fierce criticism. In so doing, it will address questions such as:

- What were the two main parties saying about the HRA in 2006?
- Why had the HRA become the focus of such controversy?
- Are recent criticisms of the HRA warranted?
- Should the HRA be left as it is, amended or replaced?

Note: Those looking for a more comprehensive introduction to the way in which the HRA and the FOI work should refer to Chapter 12 of *Annual Survey 2006*.

What were the two main parties saying about the HRA in 2006?

From spring 2006 until the end of the year, politicians of all shades could be seen lining up to lambast the HRA. For some, the problems with the Act were rooted in its very nature. For others, fault lay more in the application of the HRA than in its actual provisions. Though such politicking is common in respect of the introduction of major new pieces of legislation, these attacks were unusual in that both sides moved beyond the normal rhetoric to offer constructive proposals as to how problems with the Act might be resolved.

What promises did the government make about the HRA?

Although one would hardly expect the Labour government to abandon the Human Rights Act — given that it was the government that introduced the measure in 1998 — concerns over the way in which the Act was being applied led the government to announce a thorough review of the HRA on 14 May 2006.

It was said that this review might result in the framing of new primary legislation that could bring greater clarity to the European Convention on Human Rights (ECHR) guarantees that underpin the HRA (see Box 8.1). It was also suggested that the police and other law-enforcement and security agencies might be given further training and issued with non-statutory guidance on how precisely the HRA should be applied. Such proposals were accompanied by a series of press briefings in which Home Secretary John Reid claimed that the judges 'just don't get it' and that their rulings in respect of recent cases taken under the HRA had been prone to 'errors and misunderstandings'.

Box 8.1 Labour concern over the HRA

'In a letter from the prime minister released yesterday the home secretary, John Reid, was told to "look again at whether primary legislation is needed to address the issue of court rulings which overrule the government in a way that is inconsistent with the other EU countries' interpretation of the European convention on human rights".'

Source: Will Woodward and Clare Dyer, 'Ministers accused of reacting too quickly after promise to review human rights law', *Guardian,* 15 May 2006.

How did the Conservatives' approach to the HRA differ from that of the government?

The Conservatives, under David Cameron, took a more root-and-branch approach to the HRA, promising that the next Conservative government would 'reform, replace or scrap' the Act. Whereas Cameron agreed with the home secretary that the judges and other agencies had applied the various freedoms enshrined in the Act inappropriately, he argued that it was the Act itself — and the ECHR guarantees that it enshrined — that lay at the root of the confusion (see Box 8.2). Whereas the HRA was being used by criminals and those suspected of terrorism to evade capture and detention, Cameron argued, it had done little to protect fundamental freedoms — such as the right to trial by jury — from government encroachment.

Box 8.2 Cameron and the HRA

'We need a new approach:

- The Human Rights Act has made it harder to protect our security.

- It has done little to protect some of our liberties.

- It is hampering the fight against crime and terrorism.

- It has helped to create a culture of rights without responsibilities.'

Source: adapted from David Cameron, 'Balancing freedom and security — a modern British Bill of Rights', speech for the Centre for Policy Studies, 26 June 2006.

Thus, Cameron concluded, it might be necessary to replace the HRA with a 'modern British bill of rights' (see Box 8.3) — a codified set of rules that would properly entrench our liberties and offer a greater deal of clarity than that present in the current HRA. In favouring explicit guarantees over what Cameron called 'vague general principles', such a bill of rights would also leave senior judges significantly less room for interpretation.

Box 8.3 Cameron's bill of rights

'A modern British bill of rights:

- will define the core values that give us our identity as a free nation
- should spell out the fundamental duties and responsibilities of people living in this country both as citizens and as foreign nationals
- should guide the judiciary and the government in applying human rights law when the lack of responsibility of some individuals threatens the rights of others
- should enshrine and protect the fundamental liberties such as jury trial, equality under the law and civil rights'

Source: adapted from David Cameron, 'Balancing freedom and security — A modern British Bill of Rights', speech for the Centre for Policy Studies, 26 June 2006.

Though Cameron acknowledged that drafting such a bill of rights would involve 'huge difficulties and subtleties' and need to be founded upon a 'national consensus', he committed his party to developing the proposal during the remainder of its time in opposition.

Why had the HRA become the focus of such controversy by the summer of 2006?

Had the HRA finally entered the public consciousness?

In *Annual Survey 2006* we noted that it would take some time for the HRA to fully enter into the public consciousness (see Box 8.4). In the last year, however, matters have clearly moved on significantly in this respect. Indeed, for much of 2006, it was scarcely possible to pick up a daily newspaper without finding some reference to the Act.

Box 8.4 Adjusting to the HRA

'It will clearly take time for the rights protected by the HRA to enter the public consciousness and longer still before significant numbers of ordinary citizens are moved to employ these rights in legal action. Early cases saw the Act being used by celebrities such as Naomi Campbell, Michael Douglas and Catherine Zeta Jones, and Zoë Ball to protect their privacy, rather than by the "ordinary citizens" whom Jack Straw intended the HRA to benefit. However, recent years have seen more widespread and ground-breaking use of the Act.'

Source: Paul Fairclough, 'A new rights culture and a more independent judiciary for the UK?', in P. Fairclough, R. Kelly and E. Magee, *UK Government & Politics Annual Survey 2006* (Philip Allan Updates, 2006).

As has been the case since the HRA came into force in October 2000, such coverage has been decidedly mixed. The tabloid press continues to see it as a means by which illegal immigrants and criminals can assert their rights at the expense of the 'right-minded', 'law-abiding majority' (see Box 8.5). This focus on the HRA's supposed tendency to favour the perpetrators of crime over the victims has certainly contributed greatly to the controversy over the HRA.

Box 8.5 **The HRA in the tabloids**

'Most lawyers reckon that the [Human Rights] Act, which was passed on Mr Blair's watch, simply codifies principles, such as the right to a fair trial... that were already in English law. Its opponents disagree. As well as encouraging hijackers [see Box 8.13], they say, the Human Rights Act has given unreserved rights to murderers and made it impossible to deport criminals to countries where they might be in danger. The *Sun* newspaper, which has a Blair-like ear for public opinion, has set up a hotline for readers to call if they want to undo the Act, and has printed mugshots of troublesome judges.'

Source: 'The judges v. the government — wigging out', *The Economist*, 20 May 2006.

In the quality press, the coverage has been more measured, with the more liberal broadsheets seeing the Act as a 'good thing', in broad terms at least, and more conservative papers such as the *Daily Telegraph* and *The Times* increasingly critical of the way in which the HRA appears to tie the hands of a government seeking to ensure our safety in a changing world. The issue of public safety — specifically the question of what precisely the HRA allows the authorities to do in respect of those believed to be involved in the preparation or execution of terrorist acts — has been the main reason why the Act has become and remained so controversial. Such contingencies could hardly have been anticipated when New Labour introduced the HRA in 1998.

Even placing to one side the overall balance of press coverage, it is clear that the HRA has now become a genuine focus for debate — however 'well' informed — among the broader public. Whereas such discussions of rights and judicial action were once confined to those practitioners and commentators 'in the know', the HRA has become something about which everyone can hold an opinion.

Has the application of the HRA contributed to its controversy?
Public debate over the HRA has clearly been fuelled in no small part by the way in which the enshrined rights have been interpreted in relation to the various measures introduced since 2001 to combat the threat from terrorism.

Article 5 of the HRA protects liberty and security. Article 6 guarantees the right to a free and fair trial. Though early cases under the HRA saw such clauses used in a number of non-terrorist-related cases (see Box 8.6), the 9/11 attacks and the legislation that followed in the UK — specifically the Anti-terrorism, Crime and Security Act 2001 — drew the HRA, and those senior judges required to interpret it, into an arena that was far more politically charged.

Box 8.6 Treatment of mental patients

'A paranoid schizophrenic killer being held in Broadmoor claimed that the onus should not be on him to prove that he was no longer suffering from the condition before he could be released. Instead, it was argued, the authorities should be required to prove that he was still dangerous enough for them to detain him against his will. In requiring him to prove his health, the Mental Health Act (1983) reversed the burden of proof (protected by Article 6) and infringed his liberty (enshrined in Article 5). The appeal court agreed and ruled these provisions in the Mental Health Act incompatible with the ECHR.'

Source: adapted from Paul Fairclough, *AS & A-Level Government and Politics* (Oxford University Press, 2005).

The Law Lords' decision in December 2004 to rule the indefinite detention of suspects under clause 4 of the Anti-terrorism, Crime and Security Act 2001 incompatible with the ECHR prompted the government to rework the anti-terrorist measures that had been put in place in the wake of 9/11 (see Box 8.7). The result was the introduction of the Prevention of Terrorism Act 2005, under which the 2001 Act's provision of indefinite detention of those suspected of involvement in terrorist activity was replaced by a range of measures, including the now-infamous 'control orders' (see Box 8.8).

Box 8.7 The courts, the HRA and the detention of terrorist suspects

- The passage of the UK's Anti-terrorism, Crime and Security Act 2001, Part 4, allowed the indefinite detention, without trial, of foreign nationals whom the home secretary judged were involved in terrorism.

- This measure could be passed only because the government was able to derogate Article 5 of the Human Rights Act on the grounds that there was a 'public emergency threatening the life of the nation', which met the requirements set out in Article 15.

- In December 2004, an appellate committee of nine Law Lords ruled (8:1) that the indefinite detention of suspects under the Anti-terrorism, Crime and Security Act 2001 was, in fact, incompatible with Articles 5 and 14 of the HRA.

- In June and August 2006, the High Court found that the control orders (see Box 8.8) brought in as part of the Prevention of Terrorism Act 2005 also violated Article 5 as they were tantamount to imprisonment without trial.

Though the government had previously been advised that such measures were compatible with the HRA, senior judges found against the use of control orders in a number of cases in 2006. On 12 April, the first British Muslim placed under a control order won his appeal at the High Court, with Mr Justice Sullivan arguing that the failure to grant the accused access to the evidence justifying the control order against him limited his ability to receive a fair trial as guaranteed under Article 6. Such failings were, according to Mr Justice Sullivan, 'an affront to justice'. On 28 June, the same judge argued that a further six of the 14 control orders in force at the time were 'incompatible with human rights' because they imposed restrictions that were tantamount to imprisonment without trial, falling foul of the right to liberty and freedom guaranteed in Article 5 of the HRA.

Though rulings of this type did not oblige the home secretary to abandon control orders entirely (see Box 8.9) — even after the failure of his appeal on 1 August — they represented a serious blow to the morale of the very government that had introduced the HRA in 1998.

More significantly, perhaps, such rulings marked the point at which politicians and judges were brought into direct and often public conflict over the very basis of parliamentary statutes. This conflict — largely played out through the media in a series of increasingly blunt exchanges — clearly added to the controversy surrounding the HRA, as well as raising more serious questions regarding the independence of the judiciary.

Was the controversy over the HRA more about party politics at Westminster than the Act itself?

Though the inevitable teething problems associated with the introduction of any major piece of legislation have certainly contributed to the public debate surrounding the HRA, the Act has also become something of a 'political football' in recent months. Though the Labour government's attacks on the HRA were due in part to genuine problems and concerns regarding the way in which the Act was being interpreted and applied, they were also motivated by reasons that were, as the *Guardian* editorial of 15 May 2006 put it, 'intimately related to its own mounting political difficulties' (see Box 8.10).

Box 8.10 **Labour turns on its own creation**

'Few things in the record of the Blair government are shabbier or more destructive than its increasing tendency...to foster lies and bolster rightwing myths about its own Human Rights Act.'

Source: *Guardian,* 15 May 2006.

Similarly, many have seen Conservative attacks on the HRA as being motivated more by the prospect of party political advantage than by deficiencies in the legislation itself; it has become a suitable stick with which to beat a government on its knees. David Cameron's call for the repeal of the HRA and its replacement with a UK 'bill of rights' has drawn particular criticism in this regard (see later in the chapter) with many arguing that his proposals are so flawed as to be practically unachievable.

Are recent criticisms of the HRA warranted?

Is there a genuine problem with the very nature of the HRA, or does the problem instead lie with the ECHR or with recent anti-terror legislation?

The very nature and status of the HRA are clearly problematic. The absence in the UK of a codified constitution — allied to the supremacy of parliamentary statute — creates a situation in which the courts can issue a declaration of incompatibility only if the liberties protected under the HRA appear to have been encroached upon. For many critics, this renders the HRA a poor substitute for a properly entrenched and superior UK bill of rights. For others, the HRA goes too far, drawing senior judges into the political fray by encouraging them to challenge the very basis — as opposed to simply the application — of parliamentary statutes.

As a regular piece of statute, the HRA can be amended or repealed like any other. Under Article 15 of the ECHR, national governments are also permitted to derogate some of the convention's articles in certain circumstances. Part 4 of the UK's Anti-terrorism, Crime and Security Act 2001, for example, was passed only after the government opted to derogate Article 5 of the Human Rights Act on the grounds that there was a 'public emergency threatening the life of the nation'. This phrase, which met the requirements set out in Article 15, meant that the 2001 Act could authorise the indefinite detention — without trial — of foreign nationals whom the home secretary judged were involved in terrorism. Though things have clearly moved on in this respect since 2001, it remains the case that the HRA does not give the courts the power necessary to stop or overturn government action (see Box 8.9).

Some have moved beyond criticism of the HRA to question whether the ECHR — an agreement drawn up over 50 years ago to protect citizens against fascist states — is still relevant to the challenges posed by fascist individuals in the early years of the twenty-first century. By 9 August 2006, the home secretary, John Reid, was arguing that 'we may have to modify some of our own freedoms in the short term in order to prevent their misuse and abuse by those who oppose our fundamental values and would destroy all of our freedoms'. Such sentiments might lead one to conclude that it is the ECHR itself that needs reworking rather than the HRA, which simply makes its guarantees available to British citizens through the domestic courts.

For groups such as Justice and Liberty, however, it is what they consider to be the raft of hurriedly formulated and poorly drafted anti-terror measures placed on the statute books in the wake of 9/11 that are at the root of current problems, rather than the judges, the HRA or the ECHR. Such measures are misguided, they argue, because they strike at the very heart of our liberal democracy in a manner that is unacceptable, not only to many judges, but also to the general public (see Box 8.11).

Box 8.11 Are the anti-terror measures to blame?

'Justice, the all-party law reform group, which has officially intervened in the case, said the 2005 Prevention of Terrorism Act failed to "attain the core, irreducible minimum entitlement to natural justice" demanded by Article 6 of the European Convention on Human Rights, which spelled out the commitment to a fair trial.'

Source: *Guardian*, 4 July 2006.

Are criticisms of the police or the judges justified?

As we noted earlier in this chapter, recent criticisms of the HRA have focused as much on the way in which the Act is being applied by the police and the courts, as they have on its actual provisions. Though David Cameron's

Conservatives have been particularly vocal over the way in which the HRA has been applied — specifically the failure to strike the correct balance between the rights of the accused and the broader public interest — such

criticisms have not been confined only to the opposition benches. Senior government figures have also struggled, often unsuccessfully, to contain their frustration as Mr Justice Sullivan and others have spoken out from the bench in opposition to key elements of the government's anti-terror strategy. Though the two home secretaries who held office in 2006 (Charles Clarke — up to 5 May — and John Reid thereafter) were keen to characterise named senior judges as both confused and misguided (see Box 8.12), such friction is clearly evidence of broader changes that are under way in respect of the relationship between elected politicians and the judiciary.

Key term

Judicial independence is the principle whereby courts can operate free from political interference or control. Though judicial independence may remove some forms of bias, it does, of course, not guarantee judicial *impartiality*, as Justices retain the right to make decisions as they see fit and are protected by their security of tenure.

At the heart of this increasingly fractious relationship is the way in which each side expects the other to act. Charles Clarke provided an insight into the politician's point of view in remarks that he made in an interview in July 2006. 'One of my most depressing experiences as Home Secretary,' he explained, 'was the outright refusal of any of the Law Lords to discuss the principles behind these matters in any forum, private or public, formal or informal…It is now time for the senior judiciary to engage in a serious debate about how best legally to confront terrorism.'

While at face value such an open debate may appear to be the most constructive way forward, it is unlikely to be well received by the judiciary. Most senior judges take the view that having to justify their decisions, either publicly or privately, to government ministers would serve to undermine their independence. It is notable that the Lord Chancellor, Lord Falconer, who is well placed to see both sides of the argument, stopped short of giving credence to earlier suggestions that the government might give judges additional training on how to apply the HRA, when accepting that the police and other law-enforcement agencies might be given further guidance. Falconer also appeared to accept that the kind of public criticism of judges meted out by some of his fellow government ministers threatened the independence of the judiciary (see Box 8.13).

It is worth noting that the increasingly fractious relationship between senior politicians and senior members of the judiciary is unlikely to improve when the UK Supreme Court (created under the Constitutional Reform Act 2005) finally comes into existence.

'The Lord Chancellor insisted yesterday that Britain will not leave the European Convention on Human Rights or repeal the Human Rights Act...His defence of the Act...comes after the prime minister called a high court judge's ruling that Afghans who hijacked a plane should be allowed to stay in Britain on human rights grounds "an abuse of common sense". The judgement was branded "inexplicable" by the home secretary, John Reid.

Lord Falconer warned that criticism of the judges for their human rights rulings risked undermining judicial independence.'

Source: adapted from Clare Dyer, 'Lord chancellor defends Britain's commitment to human rights', *Guardian*, 17 May 2006.

Should the HRA be retained, reformed or repealed?

The Lord Chancellor made the government's position regarding the future of the HRA clear in May 2006 (see Box 8.13). Though he did not rule out issuing further guidance regarding the way in which the various articles of the ECHR should be applied, there would be no repeal of the HRA or withdrawal from the Convention. Essentially, therefore, the government appeared to be committed to retaining the HRA in its present form, while expressing the hope that those applying the Act would, in time, come to share the government's view of its meaning.

Repeal of the HRA and/or withdrawal from the ECHR would, in any case, be difficult, if not impossible, to execute. As Marcel Berlins noted in the *Guardian* (see Box 8.14), whereas it would be hard to repeal the HRA while leaving the ECHR in place, it would be wholly untenable for a signatory to the Convention (i.e. the UK) to pick and choose which articles it was prepared to abide by. Similarly, though remaining a party to the ECHR is not a legal requirement of EU membership, all of the 25 EU member states in 2006 were signatories.

Box 8.14 **A 'pick-and-mix' approach to the ECHR?**

'Parliament can repeal the entire Human Rights Act, but the UK would still be bound by the European Convention on Human Rights. There has been uninformed talk about "renegotiating" part of the Convention, as if it were some list which asks countries to tick the rights they are prepared to grant and put crosses next to those they do not like. To have a sort of custom-built package of rights just for the Brits is absurd.'

Source: adapted from Marcel Berlins, 'Stop blaming the Human Rights Act', *Guardian*, 15 May 2006.

More realistic is the notion that the UK might remain a signatory to the ECHR while at the same time replacing the HRA with something less open to inter-pretation. This, in a sense, is what David Cameron was hinting at with his suggestion that the UK should replace the HRA with a new bill of rights.

Although Cameron's speech introducing the proposal was intended only as the start of a lengthy process of consultation, it is interesting that he did attempt to address some of the more thorny issues commonly associated with creating such a bill of rights. On the question of entrenchment, for example, Cameron suggested that the Parliament Act could be amended in such a way as to prevent it from being used as a means of forcing through later changes to his codified UK bill of rights. Such a change would certainly be possible; after all, such a provision already exists in respect of any Commons attempt to extend the life of a parliament. Applied to a UK bill of rights, such a rule would represent a serious barrier to government encroachment, since the consent of the (as yet) unelected Lords would be required before any change to the bill of rights could be given statutory force.

Cameron also addressed the question of how his new bill of rights might operate in respect of the ECHR, arguing that his proposal — properly drafted and entrenched — would be treated sympathetically by the European Court of Human Rights in Strasbourg because it would see the bill as a genuine attempt to set out and protect core rights and values in the UK.

Conclusion

Major changes to the legal framework are invariably accompanied by teething problems. In the case of the HRA, however, such problems have clearly been made worse by the way in which the security situation has deteriorated following the 9/11 attacks. The UK is now faced with a situation in which the very government that introduced the HRA must seek to find a balance between its natural desire to see it flourish and its broader responsibility towards preserving the safety and security of UK citizens. Placing too much emphasis on individual liberties may make life easier for those seeking to 'play' the criminal justice system or — worse still — plan and carry out murderous terrorist attacks. Equally, allowing the law-enforcement and security services too much latitude may — as groups such as Justice and Liberty have argued — threaten the fundamental principles that underpin our liberal democracy.

In some respects, this is a paradox not entirely dissimilar from that facing the statesmen of the 1930s who, confronted with the unprovoked aggression of dictators such as Mussolini and Hitler, had to decide whether or not they were prepared to go to war in order to preserve the peace. Instead of issues of war and peace, however, our politicians must grapple with questions such as whether or not one should be intolerant of those who seek to challenge the UK's long-held principle of toleration, or whether a government is justified in limiting the liberties of the many in order to protect society from those few who seek to take away our liberty.

A further dimension to this debate is the way in which this tension between the day-to-day practicalities of keeping people safe and the principles of individual liberty and freedom from arbitrary arrest has served to drive a wedge between elected politicians, who often feel obliged to favour the former, and the judges, whose security of tenure and training may predispose them to act as the guardians of high principles of justice.

A similar pattern is emerging over the application of the Freedom of Information Act 2000. An inherent tension has arisen between the desire to shine a light on government and the opposing need to maintain those aspects of secrecy that help us to preserve our liberal democracy and our national security (see Box 8.15). As is often also the case under the HRA, such conflicting desires require the courts to balance individual and group rights in cases that can often be highly complex and marginal. It is difficult to see how giving in to 'knee-jerk' calls for the repeal of the HRA and the FOI would make the task of balancing such conflicting interests any easier. Instead it would run the risk of taking more power from an independent judiciary and placing it into the hands of elected politicians in whom the public is generally said to have little faith or trust.

Box 8.15 Freedom of information under attack?

In May 2006, Tony Blair argued that companies with close links to those involved in animal testing should be permitted to hide the names and identities of their shareholders. This was seen as a means of protecting those who invest in such companies from the attentions of those animal rights groups who have previously targeted them.

In July 2006, the home secretary John Reid argued for greater secrecy surrounding those who worked in and around government departments and the security services. Specifically, he argued that they should be prevented from being able to leak information using a 'public interest' defence.

Summary

- The HRA come under sustained attack from government ministers, the official opposition and the popular press alike.

- Although some of the perceived problems with the HRA appeared rooted in the Act's provisions, many commentators were also critical of the way in which senior judges were applying the HRA in their rulings.

- While the government felt that such teething problems could be overcome through the publication of further guidance on how the HRA should be interpreted, the Conservatives — under David Cameron — suggested that the Act should be replaced with a 'modern British bill of rights'.

- Some argued that the criticisms and proposals coming from both the major parties had more to do with the fact that the government was in trouble than with any faults that the HRA may have.

Chapter 9

English votes for English laws: the end of the Union?

About this chapter

Since the publication of *Annual Survey 2006*, attention has become focused on the way in which the devolution programme initiated by New Labour — particularly in respect of Scotland — has affected the relationship between nations that constitute the UK. Although the Westminster Parliament still retains control of UK foreign policy, employment regulations and the monetary system, the devolved institutions governing Scotland from 1999 were given primary legislative powers in a wide range of areas including education policy, agriculture and home affairs. This chapter focuses on the problems of legitimacy and equity resulting from such changes, on efforts to tackle these problems and on why, by the summer of 2006, some commentators were foreseeing the end of the Union. We will address key questions such as:

- Is Scotland over-represented at Westminster?

- Do we need English votes for English laws at Westminster?

- Is it time to look at the formula under which Scotland is funded?

- Can an MP representing a Scottish constituency at Westminster still aspire to become prime minister?

Are there still too many Scottish MPs at Westminster?

Although the number of Scottish MPs at Westminster was reduced from 72 to 59 ahead of the 2005 general election, the start of 2006 saw calls for the number and roles of MPs representing Scottish constituencies to be examined once more.

Taking the relative populations of the home nations into account, Scotland has traditionally been over-represented in the Westminster Parliament (see Box 9.1). In part, this is because outside the major Scottish cities, the nation's population is spread sparsely across a large geographic area. Thus, it has always been necessary to find a balance between the need to have constituencies that cover a sufficient number of constituents, while at the same time avoiding creating constituencies that are so geographically large and incoherent (socially and economically) as to be unworkable, both in administrative terms and in respect of the MPs' representative function.

How many MPs should Scotland have in the Westminster Parliament?

In the 2001 general election there were 72 Scottish constituencies. This figure was reduced to 59 in 2005. This change was made partly because of the historic over-representation of Scotland at Westminster and partly in recognition of the devolution of wide-ranging primary legislative powers to Scotland.

If seats in the Westminster Parliament in 2005 had been allocated in direct proportion to population, England would have had 541, Scotland 55, Wales 32 and Northern Ireland 18.

Interestingly, the reduction in the number of Scottish seats ahead of the 2005 general election was not simply an attempt to remedy this historic imbalance. If it had been, a similar adjustment would surely have been needed in Wales, which would have had 32 seats instead of 40. In reality, the marked reduction in the size of Scotland's voice at Westminster was instead a consequence of the creation, in 1999, of a Scottish Parliament with the kind of wide-ranging powers over primary legislation not afforded to the Welsh Assembly. It was the devolution of such powers to Scotland that had made the scale of Scotland's over-representation at Westminster appear increasingly indefensible.

Even in light of this change, however, many argue that the reduction in the number of Scottish constituencies did not go far enough. First, it is argued, the figure of 59 Scottish seats is still higher than the 55 that would have existed in 2005 if the constituencies had been apportioned between the home nations in direct proportion to population. Second, and more crucially perhaps, it is suggested that the real problem is not the number of Scottish constituencies, but the way in which the position of those elected in such constituencies has been brought into question by the creation of devolved institutions north of the Anglo-Scottish border. Such concerns were foreseen by, and have long since been encapsulated in, the so-called West Lothian Question (see Box 9.2).

What is the West Lothian Question?

The phrase 'the West Lothian Question' was coined by Enoch Powell in the 1970s as a way of summing up the concerns of the then MP for the Scottish constituency of West Lothian, Tam Dalyell.

Dalyell's concerns were over two interlocking dilemmas that might result from the programme of devolution planned by the Labour government in the 1970s:

- First, why should MPs representing Scottish, Welsh and Northern Irish constituencies at Westminster be permitted to debate and vote on measures that would no longer affect their own constituents?
- Second, is it right that such MPs would no longer have the ability to vote on matters that did affect their constituents, because such powers had been devolved to — and would therefore be discussed by — separately elected devolved institutions?

Do we need English votes for English laws in the Westminster Parliament?

Is it wrong in principle that those MPs representing Scottish constituencies can still vote on non-Scottish matters?

The West Lothian Question anticipated the problems of jurisdiction and legitimacy that might arise from a partial transfer of power to Scottish institutions. Indeed, in posing the question, Dalyell was voicing his belief that devolution would ultimately result in the end of the Union. In recent months, a series of articles in the quality press, combined with the passage of Lord Baker's Lords' Bill (see Box 9.6), have served to give the debate fresh impetus.

Though most now accept the principle that MPs returned from Scottish constituencies should not have a say on those matters that have no bearing on their own constituents, the question of legitimacy is rather more complicated than it first appears, for a number of reasons.

First, the second element of the West Lothian Question, as posed in Box 9.2, should not be taken as read. Despite the passing of primary legislative powers to devolved institutions north of the border, supreme legislative authority actually remains with the Westminster Parliament. That is to say, the right of the Westminster Parliament to legislate on Scottish matters has not been removed. Indeed, in recent months, the Westminster Parliament has increasingly sought to pass legislation that technically falls within the scope of the powers devolved to Scotland. Such measures, passed under a convention known as the Sewel Motion (see Box 9.3), came under increased scrutiny by the summer of 2006.

Box 9.3 The Sewel Motion

The Westminster Parliament can still legislate over matters within the Scottish Parliament's area of competence. This is because it retains supreme legislative power across the UK, even after devolution. In law, therefore, the UK remains a unitary, as opposed to a federal, system.

Under a convention known as the Sewel Motion, however, the Westminster Parliament will seek the consent of the Scottish Parliament for such measures. In January 2006, seven bills requiring such authorisation passed through Westminster.

According to the Constitution Unit's newsletter, *Monitor*, the 'operation of the Sewel convention has increasingly attracted criticism on the grounds that it is being used excessively, inconsistently and without sufficient scrutiny from the two parliaments'.

Second, there is the question of how precisely we may determine which areas of the UK are affected by any given measure. In reality, for example, many bills relate both to England and Wales because of the more limited powers afforded to the Welsh Assembly under the devolution settlement. In addition, though a bill may appear to have its primary focus on England, for example, it may well have an indirect — possibly even unforeseen — bearing on those who live in one or more of the other nations that comprise the Union.

Third, the way in which funds are allocated across the UK means that increases in government expenditure in one nation will have a knock-on effect for the others, as we will see when we discuss the so-called Barnett Formula later in this chapter.

Has the voting behaviour of those representing Scottish constituencies fuelled the debate?

At the time that power was handed to the devolved institutions in Scotland, many felt that MPs representing Scottish constituencies at Westminster might simply absent themselves from debates and votes on measures that had no bearing on their own constituents. The Scottish National Party went as far as to suggest that, as a party favouring full independence for Scotland, it would desist on principle from voting on English-only policies.

Despite such assurances, however, those MPs representing constituencies north of the border have been almost as active on non-Scottish issues as on matters that directly affect those who elected them. According to a report published in January 2006 by the Constitution Unit, for example, Scottish MPs voted on 61.2% of legislation that did not apply to Scotland and on 70.1% of bills that did have a bearing on their constituencies during the 2001/02 session.

Most controversial has been the position taken by many such MPs on apparently 'non-Scottish' Commons votes in which the majority of English MPs are in opposition. Particular controversy surrounded the second and third reading divisions on the bills concerning foundation hospitals (the Health and Social Care Bill) and university top-up fees (the Higher Education Bill). In all four of these divisions, the votes of those representing Scottish constituencies were crucial in passing measures that did not directly affect Scotland. In the case of top-up fees, where the only Conservative MP returned from a Scottish seat — Peter Duncan — abstained, 46 of the 54 Labour MPs representing Scottish constituencies voted in favour of the measure, five (including Tam Dalyell) voted against, two abstained, and one was absent.

In the end, the bills introducing top-up fees and foundation hospitals were passed even though there was a majority of English MPs in opposition (see Table 9.1). Speaking to the BBC after the vote, the then Shadow Education Secretary Tim Yeo argued that it was 'completely wrong that a bill which imposes higher charges on students attending the English universities should only be carried by this house using the votes of Scottish MPs when the students attending universities in the constituencies of those Scottish MPs do not have to pay those higher charges'. Duncan himself took a similarly dim view of the

line taken by many of his fellow Scottish MPs, claiming that 'the constitution-ally cavalier actions of Scottish MPs undermine the devolution settlement and play into the hands of the separatists on both sides of the border'.

	Bill	Date	All UK MPs		English MPs only		Majority against among English MPs
			For	Against	For	Against	
Foundation hospitals	Health and Social Care Bill (2nd reading)	08/07/03	286	251	217	218	1
Foundation hospitals	Health and Social Care Bill (3rd reading)	19/11/03	302	285	234	251	17
Top-up fees	Higher Education Bill (2nd reading)	27/01/04	316	311	246	261	15
Top-up fees	Higher Education Bill (3rd reading)	31/03/04	316	288	244	246	2

Source: adapted from Meg Russell and Guy Lodge, *Westminster and the English Question* (The Constitution Unit, 2005).

Table 9.1 'West Lothian' votes under Blair

Though such 'West Lothian votes' did not have as big an impact on the broader electorate as expected, they did prompt the inclusion of a commitment to 'English Votes for English Laws' (Box 9.4) in the 2005 Conservative General Election Manifesto. The fact that Labour's third consecutive term was secured with a majority of only 65 seats at Westminster — and a majority of only 44 among MPs representing English constituencies — is likely to result in a greater number of such votes in the months and years ahead.

Is the call for 'English votes for English laws' motivated by party political concerns?

The Conservatives went into the 2005 general election with a manifesto commitment to put the principle of 'English votes for English laws' in place in Commons votes. Though some have questioned the wisdom of the Conservative Party (which has traditionally been committed to the Union) unleashing anti-Scottish feeling south of the border, the proposal, unlike many of the party's other 2005 campaign pledges, was still in place at the time that this book was written.

Box 9.4 What is meant by the phrase 'English votes for English laws'?

'English votes for English laws' is the principle according to which only those MPs returned for English constituencies should be able to vote on measures solely affecting such constituencies.

There are a number of sound political reasons for the Conservatives' stance. First, the Conservative Party rarely emerges victorious from contests in Scottish constituencies. Since 1997, for example, it has never held more than one of the 72, now 59, Scottish seats (with a similarly dismal return in Wales, too). With most Scottish seats returning Labour MPs to Westminster (40 out of 59 in 2005), it is clearly Labour, not the Conservatives, who stand to lose most from any move to limit the voting rights of such MPs at Westminster.

Second, although Labour still won a majority of English seats in 2005, it did so with a smaller share of the popular vote (35.5%) in England than that secured by the Conservatives (35.7%). Senior Conservatives may well feel, therefore, that a clear focus on England and English issues has the potential to embarrass the government.

Third, the fact that two of Blair's most likely successors — Gordon Brown (Kirkcaldy and Cowdenbeath) and John Reid (Airdrie and Shotts) — represent Scottish constituencies provides a significant point of leverage ahead of a likely general election in 2009 or 2010. The question of whether or not a member representing a Scottish constituency can still aspire to the top job in UK politics is one that we will return to towards the end of this chapter.

Could 'English votes for English laws' work?

Whereas it is easy to explain why the policy 'English votes for English laws' has been so prominent in recent months, the question of whether the proposal would work is an altogether more difficult one to answer (see Box 9.5).

Box 9.5   Could 'English votes for English laws' work?

'The Conservatives' preferred policy of "English votes for English laws"...has little chance of success. It would, in effect, create a separate English Parliament within Westminster, and the potential for an elected UK government unable to legislate for England, its largest constituent part. This would cause a constitutional crisis far greater than the [West Lothian Question] itself.'

Source: press release of the Constitution Unit, January 2006.

First, there are problems of definition. Though it may be possible to identify those bills whose primary focus is on England, many will technically relate to both England and Wales. Though the devolved institutions in Wales may appear to act with a degree of independence, they do not have the powers over primary legislation afforded to their Scottish counterparts. In addition, many bills may have an indirect impact on other nations in the Union, even where this is not their primary intent. On the question of central government funding, for example, the way in which the Barnett Formula operates (see later) means that changes in funding in England will have a knock-on effect for the other home nations, even where the area of policy in question is managed

under devolved arrangements. Similarly, changes in policy in England could have unforeseen, if indirect, consequences for the other home nations. In the case of top-up fees, for example, the SNP argued that changes in the way in which universities south of the border were funded could see those in Scotland left behind. Hence, they argued, it was as reasonable for the five SNP members at Westminster to vote against the measure as it was inexplicable that 46 of those Labour MPs representing Scottish constituencies voted in favour.

Second, the practicalities of determining precisely who may participate in certain debates and divisions at Westminster might also present a more considerable obstacle than may immediately be apparent. Though Lord Baker's bill (see Box 9.6) appears simple enough in its scope and application, there would undoubtedly be considerable debate surrounding the designation of certain bills, and there would also be the question of monitoring and enforcing such changes.

Box 9.6	**Lord Baker's Bill — the Parliament (Participation of Members of the House of Commons) Bill**

This Bill was introduced in the Lords by former Conservative Cabinet Minister and Party Chair Lord (Kenneth) Baker in order to 'provide for the Speaker of the House of Commons to have power to determine the eligibility of members of the House of Commons to participate in certain legislative proceedings of that House'.

Under the Bill, the speaker would have the power to categorise bills or parts of bills according to the part or parts of the UK with which they were concerned (England, Scotland, Wales and Northern Ireland). MPs representing constituencies affected by a given measure would then be permitted to take part in debates and divisions relating to it.

Are we likely to see 'English votes for English laws' any time soon?
Although Lord Baker's Bill cleared its third reading in the Lords unopposed on 18 April 2006, it has little chance of success in the Commons as it is a private members' bill introducing a measure that the government regards as having little merit.

The Lord Chancellor, Lord Falconer, took a clear line on the Conservatives' proposal from an early stage. In a conference speech, he deliberately characterised it as a move to create a *de facto* English parliament that would mark the beginning of the end for the Union (see Box 9.7). Though the Shadow Constitutional Affairs Secretary, Oliver Heald, criticised as mischievous Falconer's efforts to portray 'English votes for English laws' as a synonym for the creation of an 'English parliament', others were quick to point out the potential pitfalls of adopting the Conservatives' proposals (see Box 9.8).

Falconer on the 'English Question'

'Speaking at a conference on constitutional reform, Lord Falconer, the Scottish-born Lord Chancellor, rejected the idea of an English parliament, suggesting that it would create two classes of MPs and break up the United Kingdom. "We would end up at exactly the point we had set out to avoid," he argued, "unbalancing the relationship between the nations. How under such circumstances could the Union survive?"'

Source: adapted from Toby Helm, 'Falconer rules out an English parliament claiming it would destroy the Union', *Daily Telegraph*, 11 March 2006.

Government by the opposition

'You cannot dodge [the question] by saying that England-only legislation would be starred in the Commons and voted on separately, but that the government would continue as before. If the Tories had a majority for most domestic policies, they would get their manifesto through — and wherever they sat in the chamber, and whatever they called themselves, they would be the lawful government of England. This thinness of the remaining non-devolved agenda, and the weakness of some kind of federal UK government, would lead to formal talks on separation within a year.'

Source: adapted from Jackie Ashley, 'If it's English vote for English law, the UK's end is nigh', *Guardian*, 12 June 2006.

Even if New Labour were convinced of the merits of the measure, it would be unlikely to lend its support to a change that would effectively reduce its Commons majority across a wide range of policy areas. The best chance of the change being adopted is, therefore, a Conservative victory at the next general election.

What are the alternatives to 'English votes for English laws'?

A further reduction in the number of MPs representing Scottish constituencies at Westminster? As noted previously, the number of Scottish constituencies was reduced from 72 to 59 ahead of the 2005 general election. Some have argued that the 'English Question' could be addressed by a further reduction in the number of Scottish seats. This might result in the total being reduced to a number in direct proportion to population (i.e. 55) or — more likely — a figure significantly lower. Thus, while the central problem of Scottish MPs voting on non-Scottish matters would remain, it would be offset to a degree by having a disproportionately small number of MPs returned from Scottish constituencies. Some may find this remedy more palatable than that of English votes for English laws, as it is less likely to lead to the emergence of the two classes of MPs referred to by Lord Falconer (Box 9.7).

The creation of an English parliament? For those who want to go beyond Lord Baker's proposal, there is always the option of creating a separate English parliament that would take on full primary legislative powers for those matters

solely relating to England. At the same time, the devolved bodies in Northern Ireland and Wales could take on similar powers, leaving the Westminster Parliament as a kind of federal legislature dealing with broader UK issues such as defence, currency, employment law and relations with the EU. Though such an option remains unpopular with voters, the Essex-based English Democrats Party claimed that support for an English parliament had risen from 16% in the 2001 British Attitudes Survey to 27% in an Ipsos MORI poll conducted along similar lines in 2006. Where respondents were first provided with contextual information on how Scottish and Welsh MPs are able to vote on English matters, their support for an English parliament rose to 41%.

Full independence for Scotland and/or dissolution of the Union? The 'nuclear option' would be clearly to grant Scotland, at least, full independence. This would have the effect of totally removing Scottish representation at Westminster. Independence remains the SNP's preferred goal, and public opinion in Scotland also appears to be moving in this direction. In a YouGov poll for the *Daily Telegraph* in June 2006, 42% of Scots said that they 'would be happy' for Scotland to become an independent country, with 40% opposing the move, and the remainder either 'not bothered one way or the other' or 'don't know'. Interestingly, however, the same poll showed that 75% of Scots believed that Scotland would remain part of the UK for 'the next 10 years or so'.

Should English taxpayers continue to subsidise Scotland?

Though the West Lothian Question is generally framed in terms of power and legitimacy, some have sought to extend the debate into the area of central government funding for the home nations. In tandem, these twin themes are now commonly referred to as the 'English Question'.

In the case of Scotland, in particular, the scope and extent of devolved powers have led to suggestions that the mechanism by which funding is allocated between the home nations should be re-worked. Such questions of funding invariably centre on the operation of the Barnett Formula (see Box 9.9). This informal arrangement, agreed in Cabinet but never given statutory footing by parliament, has been in force for nearly 30 years. Its effect is to ensure that an increase in expenditure in one part of the Union will see monies from a central fund being given to the other home nations in proportion to population — without taking into consideration existing spending, tax revenues or actual need.

Though the results of the Formula's action are widely discussed and disputed, it is often portrayed as one reason behind the widening gap between central government funding per capita in England and that in Scotland (see Table 9.2). It is no surprise, therefore, that a YouGov poll in June 2006 showed that 70% of English respondents thought that the Formula should be scrapped, whereas 74% of Scots felt that it should be retained.

The Barnett Formula

Introduced in 1978 and named after the then Chief Secretary to the Treasury, Joel Barnett, the Barnett Formula is part of the mechanism under which government spending for Scotland, Wales and Northern Ireland is determined.

The Formula works on the basis that, as a default position, a change in public expenditure in one part of the UK will result in a similar change in other areas, in proportion to their population.

The Formula works only for changes in expenditure. It does not address expenditure as a whole or the relative needs of different areas.

The impact of the Formula is disputed. Although it should result in a gradual closing of the gap between per-capita expenditure in England and that in Scotland (the 'Barnett Squeeze'), the operation of the mechanism means that a declining Scottish population can cause the funding gap to widen.

Nation	2004/05 funding		1995/96 funding
	Per capita	As % of UK	As % of UK
England	£5940	96%	96%
Scotland	£7346	119%	117%
Wales	£6901	112%	114%
Northern Ireland	£7945	129%	131%

Table 9.2 Government funding per capita in 2004/05 and 1995/96

For many commentators, the inherent unfairness in the application of the Barnett Formula was highlighted over the question of top-up fees. Under Barnett, the monies channelled into university coffers from tuition fees might be classed as additional funding in England. This change in expenditure would, it was argued, result in the Scots receiving equivalent monies from the central government, even though the Scottish Parliament had rejected top-up fees and Scottish students were not themselves required to contribute to the scheme (see Box 9.10). In essence, therefore, Scottish MPs at Westminster would have succeeded in securing additional funding for Scotland by voting to impose a new levy on English students.

Funding gain without the pain?

'Asked if he thought it was fair that Scotland should receive a windfall from the introduction of tuition fees south of the border, the Prime Minister's Official Spokesman (PMOS) said that, under the Barnett Formula, they would receive a share of additional resources. Pressed as to whether that was fair, the PMOS said [in error] that that was the Formula which had been agreed by Parliament.'

Source: Number 10 Press Briefing, 20 January 2004.

Though many would regard such an outcome as unfortunate, senior members of the government have placed a rather different spin on the link between funding and the voting rights of members representing Scottish constituencies, even turning it into an argument in favour of preserving the status quo. In a speech on 10 March, for example, Lord Falconer concluded:

> All matters — even those seemingly limited to England — impact on the Union. The funding settlement with the nations and regions of the UK means that what is decided on public funding in England, for example, affects Scotland and Wales and Northern Ireland. These are national issues for the United Kingdom and so they should be debated at the national Parliament in Westminster by all MPs, not by subsets depending on the location of their constituency.

Regardless of the debate surrounding the application of the Barnett Formula, there appears to be little political will to abolish or rework funding arrangements at present. Indeed, many fear that even talking about the per-capita gap between central government funding for Scotland and that for England may serve to fuel nationalistic or separatist tendencies within England. This was certainly the view taken by the then prime minister John Major in the 1990s (see Box 9.11).

Box 9.11 **Keeping quiet about the funding gap**

'Scotland already received 25 per cent more per head than England...I feared...that by exposing the reality of the favourable spending treatment given to Scotland, devolution would stir up latent English nationalist resentment, leading to a backlash.'

Source: John Major, *John Major — The Autobiography* (HarperCollins, 2000).

Can an MP representing a Scottish constituency at Westminster still aspire to become prime minister?

There has always been a degree of controversy surrounding the appointment of MPs representing Scottish constituencies to Cabinet posts concerned largely or exclusively with English matters (see Box 9.12). The prospect of Gordon Brown (the member for Kirkcaldy and Cowdenbeath) replacing Tony Blair as prime minister has, however, added a further dimension to the debate. In essence, the question is simple: should an MP elected by those whose own lives are governed largely by devolved bodies lead an administration that, in effect, would be governing England alone across a broad range of policy areas?

Certainly, the YouGov poll for the *Daily Telegraph* in June 2006 would not have given a good deal of room for optimism (see Table 9.3). Offering the choice of two statements, the survey would appear to highlight a real problem for the Labour Party in the run-up to a general election in 2009 or 2010. Most worryingly, perhaps, is the fact that 10% of those who had previously indicated that they were intending to vote Labour agreed with the second statement — that those representing Scottish constituencies should be barred from becoming prime minister.

Box 9.12 A problem for Gordon and John?

'One recurring controversy revolves around the appointment of Scottish MPs to ministerial posts with a predominantly English workload. Home Secretary John Reid has come under fire in the Tory press on these grounds even though his portfolio includes major all-UK policy matters such as asylum, immigration and terrorism policy. More worrying for the government (or at least its Chancellor) is that questions have also been asked of whether a Scottish MP could now legitimately become prime minister. Shadow Cabinet member Alan Duncan suggested this would be "almost impossible" though he was swiftly slapped down by party leader David Cameron.'

Source: *Monitor*, September 2006.

A Westminster MP for a Scottish constituency should be able to become United Kingdom prime minister.	56%
A Westminster MP for a Scottish constituency should be barred from becoming United Kingdom prime minister.	25%
Don't know.	19%

Table 9.3 Results of a YouGov poll for the Daily Telegraph, *June 2006*

This is a particular concern, given that one of Brown's supposed rivals for the top job, John Reid, also represents a Scottish constituency (Airdrie and Shotts). Such results may help to explain Brown's efforts to show his backing for the English football team in the 2006 World Cup — support that only one-third of those asked regarded as genuine — and also his efforts to champion the notion of 'Britishness'. It might also explain why some in the party were looking to push the merits of other contenders, such as Education and Skills Secretary Alan Johnson, by the time of the Labour Party Conference in September.

Box 9.13 The West Lothian Question re-energised

'The West Lothian Question has been fashioned into a dagger pointed at Labour's legitimacy and at a future Brown-led administration… The Chancellor's campaign to investigate and propagate the values of Britishness…seems too much like special pleading by a Scot worried about his own future role.'

Source: adapted from Jackie Ashley, 'If it's English vote for English law, the UK's end is nigh', *Guardian*, 12 June 2006.

Conclusion

Although the West Lothian Question was originally born of genuine concerns regarding a proposed scheme of devolution, the debate has clearly become rather more pointed in recent years (see Box 9.13). In part, this transformation has arisen because commentators have been able to examine the results of the changes made following Labour's return to government in 1997, as opposed to simply speculating about the consequences that devolution might bring. One should not, however, underestimate the role played by Westminster party politics in re-energising and refocusing the debate. Though the consequences of introducing a scheme of English votes for English laws are so far-reaching as to make even most Conservatives pull back from the brink, there is still a good deal of political capital to be had from floating the idea, if only to make life difficult for Blair's most likely successor.

Summary

- Tam Dalyell's fears regarding devolution, encapsulated in the 'West Lothian Question', have largely been borne out by events since the establishment of devolved government in Scotland in 1999.

- The questions of legitimacy and representation, which are at the heart of the West Lothian Question, associated with ongoing concerns over Scotland's favourable funding arrangements (specifically the operation of the Barnett Formula), have seen the emergence of what some have termed the 'English Question'.

- Though none of the proposals to tackle this 'English Question' — including the call for English votes for English laws — provides a wholly satisfactory solution, the question itself has afforded the Conservative Party a means of questioning the legitimacy of Labour's government of England.

- Gordon Brown's chances of succeeding Tony Blair as prime minister have been affected by a growing feeling that those returned to Westminster from Scottish constituencies should be barred from holding certain senior offices that have no direct bearing on their own constituents.